THE PSYCHOLOGY OF THE PERSON

THE PSYCHOLOGY
OF THE PERSON

Neville Symington

KARNAC

First published in 2012 by
Karnac Books Ltd
118 Finchley Road
London NW3 5HT

British Library Cataloguing in Publication Data

A C.I.P. for this book is available from the British Library

ISBN-13: 978-1-78049-069-4

Typeset by Vikatan Publishing Solutions (P) Ltd., Chennai, India

Printed in Great Britain

www.karnacbooks.com

For James and Penny

CONTENTS

ACKNOWLEDGEMENTS

There are too many people to acknowledge. My understanding of the person finds its origin in the way I was treated by my mother and father, later the inspiration I gained from certain teachers at my first little school in Oporto, then later at public school in England, and yet later when I was at college. Inspiration is the right word. I was lucky enough to have teachers at every educational grade who lit up a flame of enthusiasm inside me and to all of them I am deeply grateful.

I have a particular debt to John Klauber who was my analyst when I was doing the analytic training. He "saw" me and, more than seeing me, he believed in me. He saw who I was and did not try to slot me into some impersonal system of thinking.

This book is an expansion of a series of lectures which I gave at the Tavistock in June 2009 and organised by Jane Ryan of Confer. I owe thanks to many in the audience who contributed and broadened my understanding. In particular Gilit Hurvits who was present and who also has looked at the central things I have written and made helpful comments. There were others in the audience, like my old friend and colleague Isca Wittenberg, with whom I had significant conversations. I would also like to thank David Shulman who has looked over some of the chapters. It was listening to his paper on "Imagination" in October of the year 2005 that I first saw how the creative act has a transitive function, and I would also like to thank my colleague Gabi Mann who initiated this fruitful contact.

I would like to thank Mrs Jan Campbell-Thompson who went through all the chapters, which was a laborious business and removed repetitions and indicated correctly where further explanation was indicated. It was a work that took her a serious amount of time and without it I could not have produced the book.

ABOUT THE AUTHOR

Neville Symington is a psychoanalyst in private practice in Sydney, Australia. As a young man he took a diploma in philosophy and then in theology. He later did a degree in psychology and took a diploma in clinical psychology. He did his psychoanalytic training in London and is a fellow of the British Psychoanalytic Society. He held a senior staff position in the adult department of the Tavistock Clinic from 1977–1985. He was also chairman of the psychology discipline for the adult and adolescent departments at the Tavistock Clinic in London. In 1986 he migrated to Sydney, Australia where he was chairman of the Sydney Institute for Psychoanalysis from 1987–1993. He was president of the Australian Psychoanalytical Society from 1999–2002. He is the author of *The Analytic Experience* published by Free Association Press and St. Martin's Press, of *Emotion and Spirit* published by Cassell and later re-published by Karnac Books, of *Narcissism: A New Theory, The Making of a Psychotherapist, The Spirit of Sanity, A Pattern of Madness, How to Choose a Psychotherapist, The Blind Man Sees, A Healing Conversation,* and *Becoming a Person through Psychoanalysis,* which are all published by Karnac Books. He is joint author with Joan Symington of *The Clinical Thinking of Wilfred Bion* published by Routledge. He also published a novel called *A Priest's Affair* published by Free Association

Press and a book of poetry *In-gratitude and Other Poems* published by Karnac.

In 2007 he started a clinical organisation called Psychotherapy with Psychotic Patients (PPP). It had its first conference in February 2010 with Michael Robbins as keynote speaker together with himself and Jim Telfer. He has lectured in Britain, Norway, Denmark, Poland, Portugal, Germany, the United States, Brazil, Israel, India, Japan, New Zealand, and Australia. He has a website at: www.nevillesymington.com.

INTRODUCTION

In this book I attempt to sketch out a "Psychology of the Person". The definition of "person" implies that no two people, even identical twins, are the same. Although this is obvious and no sensible person would quarrel with such a view, yet many terms are used that imply that there is a sameness between two or more people. For instance, it is often said that one individual is *identified* with another, which in ordinary language means that he or she makes him or herself the *same* as the other, yet this is an impossibility. As Vasily Grossman says, "Everything that lives is unique. It is unimaginable that two people, or two briar-roses, should be identical ..." (1995, p. 19). Yet the word *identify* or *identification* is used so often that it seems to be a valued ideal that people, amazingly different, should be pressed together into one lump of stuff. It is a fact that an author belonging to one school of thinking will frequently quote from authors from the same school of thinking, people all carved out of the same block of material. Kleinians nearly always quote from their fellow Kleinians, self psychologists from their own school, and so on.

If I cannot rely on the assumptions of a particular school of thinking then how am I to know the inner life of another and enter into sympathetic relation with him or her? The quick answer is that to be able to do so requires me to be a person. So what is a person? How is a person different from someone who is not a person? A revolution occurs and suddenly here is a person in front of me and he begins to speak of the horror of his previous state as a robot. What is it that has occurred? If it were possible to X-ray his soul what would the emotional radiologist see now which was not present before?

This book sets out to answer these questions. I try to formulate a "Psychology of the Person". I don't think this has been done before. The relational school has investigated the problem at a practical clinical level but, because I think the abrogation of the person both within psychoanalysis and within psychology has been so widespread, it is necessary to get to grips with the problem at its core. I am reminded of G. K. Chesterton's take on what is required when a social disease requires diagnosis:

> If your aeroplane has a slight indisposition, a handy man may mend it. But, if it is seriously ill, it is all the more likely that some absent-minded old professor with wild white hair will have to be dragged out of a college or laboratory to analyse the evil. (1910, p. 11)

I am certainly old enough, absent-minded enough to qualify for the post of analysing what constitutes a person. I neither have white hair nor any professorial status so I put forward my thesis with the hope that it may stimulate a true professor to come forth and correct and amplify what I have written here. There have been scholarly books such as Rom Harré's Personal Being (1983) with its carefully introduced distinctions, but what I want to do here is to paint in colours, scarlet and black, what constitutes a person and what does not. I hope by doing this it will evoke better answers than I have been able to give as Daniel Dennett suggests in his theory of consciousness: "There are still plenty of mistakes in the theory I will offer here, and I hope they are bold ones, for then they will provoke better answers by others" (1993, p. xi). I am sure at present there are background assumptions which blind us to personhood. It is these background assumptions that I want to highlight with a beam of white light and replace them with ones which justly honour the reality of the person. The person is a challenge to any theory that tries to homogenise people according to a principle that does not have sufficient abstraction to accommodate differences both between individual people and also within the composite of the individual him or herself.

That remarkable but forgotten thinker Macneile Dixon says:

> The most troublesome thing in the world is the individual man ... There are vehement and hot-headed men, selfless and conciliatory men. There are sybarites and ascetics, dreamers and bustling active men of affairs, clever and stupid, worldly and religious, mockers and mystics, pugnacious, loyal, cunning, treacherous, cheerful, and melancholy men. (1958, p. 171)

I quote this in order to emphasise his use of the word *troublesome*. He should of course have said *men and* women. The person is a trouble to dictatorial regimes but also to all schools of thinking that try to fit the human person into a system. This is something the person will not allow. The modern disease is the one that reduces the single person into a nondescript unit according to an orderly uniformity. Martin Buber noted this long ago: "... in this idea of the social life two basically different things are combined—first, the community that is built up out of relation, and second, the collection of human units that do not know relation—modern man's palpable condition of lack of relation" (1987, p. 137). This condition where there is a lack of relation is written into the language and theories in psychology, in psychoanalysis, and in social psychology. I hope that one fruit of this book will be to heighten awareness of those theories and models which implicitly incur the banishment of the person.

.

CHAPTER ONE

Analysis creating the person

ive years ago I spent a day in the acute ward for adolescents in a psychiatric hospital. At the end of the day a woman member of the staff, Jocelyn, came up to me and asked if she could come to see me for a single session. Two days later she arrived. She was in her mid-thirties, had been married for eleven years and had two young children, a boy and a girl of eight and six. She was in despair. Her husband waited upon her for all decision making. Where were they to go on holiday? It was *she* who had to decide. Which school should our daughter go to?—it was *she* who had to decide. Should we move house? He did not know, *she* had to decide. When they were going to visit her parents he asked her what subjects he should talk to them about. In exasperation she told him that she had to leave him; that she could bear it no longer. "Please explain what you mean?" he asked her. Jocelyn tried to explain, so he said, looking at her with pleading eyes, that he would try harder but "Please tell me what to do?" There was something very sad about it; he sounded a good man, he loved his children, loved his wife but where was the *I* who feels, who desires, who makes decisions, who makes judgments, who yearns, who loves? It must have suited his wife when she married him but she had grown, something was unfolding in her, she had begun to be her own person and now she wanted *personhood*

1

in the figure of her husband, not a clone of herself. A relating *I* was bursting out of an enclosed egg. In the interview she looked to me to see whether leaving her husband was the right thing to do. So there was a relic of her cloning husband inside her (needing me to tell her whether she should leave her husband) but the free her had dawned and the "follow-my-leader" side had shrunk.

How are we to understand her husband's problem? There seemed to be no *I* within him. I have had several patients suffering from this condition within the last decade. It is common for me to hear a patient saying: "I am feeling depressed but I am glad that I am feeling it," or: "I felt angry when you finished the session yesterday but it's a relief that I feel it." A man came to see me whose wife had died in a tragic accident ten years earlier and he told me that he knew it was sad but that he did not feel it. What is common to all these cases is the absence of an *I* who feels. Sometimes it takes a more restricted form. So a man who is a playwright said I know that what I write is good but I don't feel it.

Treating people in this condition has convinced me that the *I* is there potentially in everyone but in some people it has not grown. The image that comes closest to the absent *I* is of a jelly slopping around but there is nothing to hold it together—there is no *I*. Yet there is some innate desire, or even urgent need, to have a togetherness, so a common solution is to find an outer mould into which this sloppy jelly can be poured. So, for instance, a man, who had read many psychoanalytic books, said that he was now mature and securely attached but his behaviour belied it; sexually he was hither and thither and all over the place. So if there is this innate desire born of an inner knowledge why has it not developed into an interior coherence? There is a seed that has not been watered or given sunlight. The sense I have is that this little nugget of potential is looking for an environment where it can grow, develop and become so that the goal of the therapeutic procedure is not in healing a wound or knocking down defences but in building an *I* which has never been there. The task is to bring an infant into adulthood; to create the *I*. The job of an analyst, a therapist, or any human helper is not to repair what has been damaged but to create what has not yet come to be.

We have a theory that there is an *I* which avoids certain events because they are painful but this assumes that there is a fully fledged *I* that could face or bear the pain. This leads to a covert moralism. The assumption here is that the *I* is not yet formed. The psycho-analyst's task is to form the *I*. A patient said to me: "I think Descartes had it wrong. It is not 'I think therefore I am' but '*You* think therefore I am'." The belief here is that one person thinking about the other brings about the the birth of *I*.

There are two ways in which any element can exist within the personality. It can be present either uncreated or created.[1] The task of psychoanalysis is to create the uncreated, to create what is already there. I shall give some examples to explain what I mean. Gravity existed before Isaac Newton, yet he created it—he created what was already there. He did not impose anything upon the universe and he did not just find it. He is hailed as a genius because from his observations and calculations he fashioned something, he created a reality which was already there. This is a difficult concept to grasp. Another way of trying to understand it is that of the condition of *agnosagnosia*, when someone does not know that either an amputated limb or a dysfunctional limb is as it is but believes it to be still a fully functional limb. This occurs when there has been damage to the right side of the brain to which the creative mental faculty is partnered. It is through the right hemisphere that the creative work occurs. The mind-brain partnership is not able to create what is there when there has been damage to the right hemisphere. This suggests that I only know that my hand is my hand, my leg is my leg, my arm is my arm if I have created what is already there—that I do not know it until that creative act has occurred. I encountered a patient who did not know that his hand was *his* hand but needed his psychotherapist to tell him so. So, in the case of *agnosagnosia*, when a limb has been amputated the creative function is no longer possible so the individual so afflicted cannot know that his limb has been amputated. The original creation of a functional limb cannot be reversed. The artist who painted the picture has died so he cannot restore his painting. To know that I have a limb which has been amputated I have to create what is there. If when I was creating I had an undamaged left arm then that is what I know because I have created it but if my creative source is impaired at the time when I have my left arm amputated then I am left with what was created before that event. I know it through creating. I cannot know what I have not created.

This was the great insight of Giambattista Vico who taught that we have a special knowledge of that which we have created. Whereas Descartes had thought that we know best the uncreated world of nature, Vico said that these are only sensed from their outside. Only God, said Vico, can know them because he made them, he created them. We humans can only know that which we have created, and I extend this insight of Vico's even to our own bodies. This is the importance of realising that even what is there needs to be created. The third analogy is from the condition of autism whose root I believe is the same as in the case of *agnosagnosia*. The autistic child (and autistic adult) does not relate to his mother or to others and this is because the relation has not been created. The connecting link between one human and another also has to be created just as the limbs of the body also have to be created. When this creative function is defective then the relation is not created and we have the condition known as *autism.* The right side of the brain and this *formative power* of the mind are in a close partnership and if this is not functioning then the givens we are born with cannot become us; my hand cannot become mine, that woman cannot become my mother. The fourth analogy is a clinical example: a woman's mother died when she was fifteen years old; she was now aged thirty-one. Her mother's death was a biographical fact and she spoke of it as though it were about someone of remote significance to her, but then she had a dream where she was flying like a bird over the home of her birth and she looked down and saw a funeral procession leaving the house and she knew her mother was in the coffin. She had now created the event of her mother's death. She now knew her mother had died not just objectively but sub-jectively. Dreaming as a creative power rather than an instinctual wish fulfilment, as Freud saw it, was central in the thinking of Wilfred Bion who used the term *alpha function* to describe this. So the clinical problem is how do we proceed if this creative function is undeveloped?

Consciousness is a product of this inner creative activity. Conscious-ness means I know something now which I did not know before. We are all familiar with that sentence: "I knew before but now I know that I know." The inner creative activity is primary; consciousness is secondary. This inner unseen creative activity produces consciousness. This creative activity brings disparate elements together into a pat-tern; unity is at the core of consciousness. If something is unconscious it is because the something that is there has not been created, there is a scatter of elements and this is the reason why they are unconscious. The creative function works upon the disparate elements bringing them into a unity. Long before Isaac Newton, people had seen apples fall-ing from trees, rivers pouring their waters down mountainsides into the sea, animals held to the earth and not floating in the air, the moon circling the earth, the planets circling the sun. In a creative act Newton determined an inner unifying principle. He called this principle gravity. In an analogous way the disparate elements in the personality become the material of a creative act which unifies them.

Consciousness may be either not present or very restricted. This may be because the creative function is undeveloped or because to create it burdens the personality with the pain of loneliness. These two intersect and I hope to show how this function can grow and expand. Other pains come with that: guilt, shame, disappointment, or sadness. Loneliness is primary and consciousness of it is the subjective registration of person-hood being born.

We need to consider what are the conditions necessary for this creative function to flourish. The right hemisphere is where the creative function is partnered in the brain so that damage here disables the creative function. What though is the mental correlate of the right side of the brain? Do we need to think of the creative function as a seed which has to be fostered and if so who or what is it that does the fostering?

We turn first to the research into early mother-infant bonding. I start with a quote from Peter Hobson:

> The person who is free to evaluate attachments is able to assimilate and think about her own past experiences in relationships, even when these have been unsatisfactory. She has mental space to relate to her own relations with others. She can reflect on her own feelings and impulses and can forgive and tolerate her own shortcomings. So, too, she has space to relate to her own baby as an independent and separate person and to be sensitive to her baby's states of mind in such a way that the baby is likely to become securely attached. (2002, p. 178)

When the mother's own essence—her *in-relation*—is present it brings to birth the same essence in her baby. What we need to look at here is what is meant by "securely attached". The link between one individual and another is either by "attached proximity" or by "intuitive connection". The former is from the outside whereas the latter is from within. The former was called "adhesive identification" by Esther Bick (1986, p. 62). Martin Buber has referred to it as *differentiation through pure juxtaposition* (1987, p. 38). The latter comes from an act of understanding that comes from within. We need therefore to penetrate into the act of understanding and see, as far as we can, what it is, what constitutes the act of understanding. There is an indwelling and embracing that fashions the act of understanding. But what is it that does the indwelling? What is it that does the embracing?

We have here to decide whether there is any substance in the world that is immaterial. I take the stance that woven into the world of physical objects there are relations between events that are real but not detectable because they are not material. This has been expressed succinctly by a Canadian philosopher, Peter March (2004):

> If the mind were a system of physical relations between material objects then, in a sense, the mind would not be visible. Consider first the very simple relation "in front of". Let's take the example where someone says that one of her hands is in front of the other. It is true, in a sense, that this relation between two objects is not itself visible—in the sense in which the objects themselves are visible. The relation exists, of course, but if we were asked to give the colour or the shape of the relation we would be stumped. So, granting that we do say that we can see that someone is in front of another person and granting further that most physical relations are discovered using visual information, still, since they have neither colour nor shape, they violate our intuition which suggests that everything which can be seen in the primary sense must have colour and shape.
>
> In another sense these relations are invisible because the relevant relata are not easily observable. One can say that it is a visible fact that one hand can be seen to be in front of the other. But the relations of mind exists as relations between neural structures of the person and objects which are not part of the person's body, hence, and since these relata are not visible to the naked eye, the relations themselves are not visible. We can not see that one hand is in front of another if we can't see one of the hands.
>
> What this means is that if the mind is a system of relations then we would be unable to give its colour or its shape, nor would we be able to detect the relevant relations by sight.

One can think of these *relata*, as Peter March calls them, as both embracing and indwelling. This in-between-ness of the two hands both embraces both hands and, at the same time, dwells within each hand. This relationship is not material. So I take my stance that there is a non-material quality that interpenetrates the universe. It is this interpenetration occurring between two people becoming conscious in the act of understanding.

In another place I have referred to "attached proximity" or "differentiation by pure juxtaposition" as "glue-like attachment" (Symington, 2002, pp. 80–81). It is an attachment to the other as of surface to surface and here there is no relation, no embracing, no indwelling. I use the term *glue-like attachment* in order to indicate that the juxtaposition is one that is fiercely gripped. I use *glue-like* rather than *adhesive* as it is closer to a picture or image that carries emotional power. Freud, in his theoretical exposition, did not differentiate the way in which we come to knowledge of human beings from the way in which we come to knowledge of the non-human world. We process stimuli coming from outside us through the senses. The ego, he said, processes the stimuli from the outer world (and inner world) without any differentiation. It is the same process whether the outer object is a rock, a building, a tortoise, or a human being. However, Freud was honest and so noted instances that were an exception to this like:

> I have good reason for asserting that everyone possesses in his own unconscious an instrument with which he can interpret the utterances of the unconscious in other people. (Freud, 1913i, p. 320)
>
> It is a very remarkable thing that the Ucs. of one human being can react upon that of another, without passing through the Cs.
>
> This deserves closer investigation, especially with a view to finding out whether preconscious activity can be excluded as playing a part in it; but, descriptively speaking, the fact is incontestable. (Freud, 1915e, p. 194)

But he never made a theory to support his knowledge that an activity of this sort does occur between human beings. The result is that there is a theoretical scaffolding that supports *glue-like attachment* but not *connection through intuition*. So, for instance, a man said to me: "Your interpretations are not correct but I know you are trying to understand and it is that which matters to me." When he said he knew that I was trying to help him I do not think he was trying to temper his criticism so as to find favour with me. So how does he *know* that I am trying to understand? It is not that I have said to him: "I am trying to understand you,

you know." He does not know it through words. He has some faculty that reaches from his heart to my heart. There is a penetration into me. Some mind-stuff of his dwells in my mind-stuff.

Another way of approaching this is to analyse the act of understanding. Someone is trying to explain something to me but I don't get it. Then they put it another way and I still don't get it and then he makes a chance remark and suddenly I grasp it. I grasp it from a place in me that is non-verbal. The act of understanding does not lie in the words that my friend was using explain it. They are pointers *towards*. But *towards* what? An experience. The pointer has to be close enough to the experience for me to be able to grasp it. Yet in the act of understanding there is a new element. The struggle is in two parts. I have within me a collection of acts of understanding and they are a deposit within me. So one task I am engaged in is searching for a particular one. I have had an act of understanding and it informs my way of relating to the world but my attention needs to be called to it. The words are like names put on files. Naming of files is so that a particular content can be easily found. When my friend is using different words I cannot find the content to start with because it is not the name in which the particular experience-content has been filed. When suddenly the chance remark brings me to the right file it is because it is the right name for the file or that it is close to it. Does this mean that all the contents are already there and it is just a question of finding them? Can no new content be added to the store which is already there? There are two answers to this: one is that a new experience can occur and secondly a greater abstraction embraces what is there but in a deeper way.

I shall take the first one first. I will start with an example that comes from Tolstoy's novel *Anna Karenina* (1877). Anna is about to give birth to a baby which she has conceived with Vronsky. Karenin, Anna's husband, is on his way home to Anna from Moscow to St. Petersburg. He hates Anna and hopes that she will die. Then when he sees her and attends the birth he changes and becomes filled with love for her and Tolstoy comments: "… it was not until he saw his dying wife that he knew his own heart." In his own heart was a love for her but was it there before he saw his wife dying? There is the implication in Tolstoy's comment that seeing his wife dying (in fact she does not die then but he does not know that) brings to birth a love in his heart which he did not know was there. But was it there? The answer is yes and no. It needed the experience of seeing his wife dying to make it known to him. It is like the watering of a dry seed. The experience of seeing his wife dying brings it to birth. There is an intercourse between his heart and the outer event which gives birth to an emotion we know as love. So there is the event which is both inner and outer. It can then be named. Karenin might have called it "death emotion" and he may not understand someone trying to explain to him the way the inner and outer are connected until by chance he says, "It's like the distress at someone's death," and suddenly Karenin grasps it when all the previous attempts to explain with philosophical terms failed. So then here is the re-finding of the experience. Can something further or new come about? Or are we saying that it is all potentially there and that it needs an experience to bring it to birth, to make it real? Can another person's experience add to my own? What I am trying to get at here is, "Can I enlarge my understanding through the experience of another?" I think the answer is yes but only if there is desire in the person—i.e., if there is desire to expand one's experience; to open ourselves to the world of which we are a small part. The other can give to me his experience through my own act of understanding but there has to be a closeness for it to occur. My own act of understanding brings within me the experience of another. There is a mutual indwelling of one in the other. It is that mind-stuff has the capacity to dwell within the other and to receive the other within it. The symbol for this mutual indwelling lies in the sexual act where the penis enters the vagina and the vagina receives into itself the penis. Mind-stuff has this plasticity that enables mutual indwelling. Understanding is the conscious consequence of this invisible happening. I will take an example from the approach of Isaiah Berlin as opposed to that of Michael Polanyi in relation to our understanding of the world.

Isaiah Berlin, basing himself on the insights of Giambattista Vico, believed that the way in which we know the inanimate world is different from the way in which we know our fellow human beings: that there is a different form of knowledge. We have knowledge of human beings from the inside whereas our knowledge of the non-human world is from the outside. We can know what it is like to be John Smith in a way that we can never know what it is like to be a tortoise, a wasp, a tree, or a stone. This was the position taken by Isaiah Berlin but Michael Polanyi says that this differentiation fails to take account of the nature of the act of understanding. He says that understanding rests upon a certain indwelling of the mind in the object and therefore he says there is a certain indwelling of the mind even in inanimate nature, whereas with other human beings it has reached a higher level of operation but that the act itself is similar. If I understand Polanyi correctly he means that when Archimedes enjoyed that famous moment in the baths of Syracuse when he came to know volume this was the consequence of a certain indwelling. This is a good illustration because this moment of insight happened as he was lowering his body into the waters and noticing the water which his body displaced. The sensual physical happening is in one place and the mind-concept of volume is in another and there is a leap from the physical to the mental but there is a certain sympathetic similarity. There is the notion here that the mental event transcends the bodily happening. So also, I believe that the act of understanding is not just the product of a mutual indwelling but also transcends it; takes it to a new dimension. The indwelling is within the being-ness of the act.

However, I believe that Isaiah Berlin is right because the indwelling between one human being and another is reciprocal whereas between a human being and the non-human world it is not. There is a capacity for indwelling within another human being which is not so with the non-human world so that the indwellingness goes both ways when it is another human being.

* * *

When an element in the personality is uncreated the individual is ruled by it; when it is created the person is both lived in it and, at the same time, lives it. The person lives it as a process; he does not govern it as a possession. If that process is infused with a third term of a particular kind then the two poles of the process become persons.[2] The third term needs to be infinite for this process to occur. The process is captured through static images. The fixed quality of these images is on account of a function in the personality that *fixes* them. It is the intelligence[3] which does the fixing. It produces a snapshot. The snapshot is initially a sensual image which is static and this is then denuded of the sensual aspect and thus becomes a concept. No one emphasised this more than Henri Bergson who says of intelligence,[4] "… always engaged as it is in determining under what former heading it shall catalogue any new object" (1919, p. 51), and again in another passage:

> … the intellect represents *becoming* as a series of *states*, each of which is homogeneous with itself and consequently does not change.

Is our attention called to the internal change of one of these states? At once we decompose it into another series of states, which, reunited, will be supposed to make up this internal modification … though we may do our best to imitate the mobility of becoming by an addition that is ever going on, becoming itself slips through our fingers … the intellect lets what is *new* in each moment of a history escape. It does not admit the unforeseeable. It rejects all creation. (Bergson, 1919, pp. 171–172)

Bion refers to this as the progress from a conception to a concept which he defines thus: "The concept is derived from the conception by a process designed to render it free of those elements that would unfit it to be a tool in the elucidation or expression of truth" (1963, p. 24). The static objectified image in the personality is called *me*; the processing source is called *I*. The processing source has within it two faculties: an operation of the senses and an operation of the intellect.[5]

Once the intelligence has fixed the process in a concept the personality is in the grip of this concept; if the personality is in a broken state it imprisons the *I*-process in it. A static concept is uncreated as soon as it entraps the *I*-process.[6] It is created when the intelligence is servant to the *I*-process. Because the conception, in Bion's terms, has sensual elements it has a magnetism which fastens the *I* to it. This means that it will distort the truth because the *I* is conditioned then by this attachment.

So the uncreated can be of two forms. Either it can be something that is received into the personality, bypassing the *I*-process or something that has been created by the *I*-process but then the *I*-process is imprisoned within it. Although created by the *I*-process it has now become a prisoner within the personality. This means that there is something in the personality that is capable of objectifying that which has been created.

The subjective signal that this has happened is excitement. Marion Milner gives a good example of this:

I was one day driving over the mountain road to Granada in the spring, the cone-shaped red earth foothills all covered with interlacing almond blossom. Also it was the first sunny weather after days of rain. I was filled with exultation as we climbed higher and higher into the clean mountain air. I was full of that kind of exultation which makes one above oneself, I felt powerful and important as if it was somehow my doing that the country was so lovely. Or at least that I was cleverer than other people in having got myself there to see it. I was certainly thankful that I was not as other men are. Then I noticed that the character of the country was changing but as soon as I tried to look back in my own mind I found there was nothing there only a rather absurd memory of my own exultation but no living vision of what had caused it. Then I remembered the pharisee and the publican … At once the look of the country was different. I was aware only of it, not of myself at all. And always afterward there was that bit of Spain that I seem to possess in my imagination. (Milner, 1937, pp. 208–209)

So the sensual element, on condition that the *I* is in a state of isolation, is capable of *ecstasising* the *I*. Sexual orgasm is just an extreme case of something that is present in all sensual attachments. It is why mystics have emphasised the need of detachment from the senses. Also the emphasis among those who have studied attachment upon the requirement that the mother be able to reflect is another angle on the same point. The mother who is able to reflect is therefore not ruled by an attachment to a painful or pleasurable sensual memory. She is detached from the experience. That capacity to reflect means that the *I* is detached from the sensual and is now governed by that other operation in the *I*-process: the intellect. This is different from the intelligence which makes static what is in movement. The intellect grasps the *all-inclusive principle* but not the particular. Imagery whether through art, poetry, or music captures the particular; the intellect can only ever capture what is general.

The creative is an animating principle that governs the imprinting whether that comes from an outer or inner stimulus. It is something that Picasso referred to as a metaphorical inner eye that endows the senses with something which they lack: the capacity to see and feel emotionally (Penrose, 1971, pp. 91–92).

In the first case the individual is psychically dead; in the second she is alive and is a person. The two words I shall use here to distinguish between them are the *individual* and the *person*.

A state of madness exists when someone is lived by uncreated elements. This is what is meant by madness: that there is no inner all-inclusive principle governing what occurs. Sanity is when the stimuli have been infused with the medicine from that inner eye.

The purpose of this book is to investigate whether psychoanalysis is able to transform the *individual* into a *person* and if so how.

I believe that psychoanalysis is able to transform madness into sanity under certain conditions and allowing for certain restrictions. Our purpose in this book is to try to show that this is possible.

Notes

1. The connection between this distinction and Bion's *beta elements* and *alpha elements* is evident.
2. This "third term" is examined in detail in Chapter Nine.
3. A distinction is made in this book between *intelligence* and *intellect*.
4. He uses the term "intellect" (in the English translation at least) but is referring to what I have here called "intelligence".
5. See footnote 12.
6. I think this projection of oneself into the conception is what Bion means by it becoming saturated.

CHAPTER TWO

A creative principle

The proposition is this: that there is in every human being a creative principle. This principle is not known directly but rather indirectly. We infer such a principle therefore from its manifestations. Marion Milner puts this clearly when talking of how artists depict nature:

> I began to suspect that they were in fact trying to describe the process of surrendering themselves to the deep spontaneous responses of nature within them, that were stimulated by the contact with nature outside of them. (1987, pp. 222–223)

So what she is saying here is that the "nature outside of them" gave them a picture of what was inside of them. When the function of these manifestations is to point and reveal the invisible inner principles we name them symbols.

The fact that it cannot be known directly is synonymous with saying that it is unconscious—i.e., we are not aware of the thing itself but infer it through things that point to its presence. This is not primarily because the personality defends against it but because the mind is geared to objects but cannot take its own source of activity as an object directly but only indirectly. This ability of the mind to represent one thing by another is the great mutation which took place in the latter part of the process of *hominisation*.

The importance of this mutation cannot be overemphasised. Palaeontologists refer to it as the *upper/middle palaeolithic transition*. This refers to that moment between 60,000 and 40,000 years ago when early modern humans began to make representations of objects. *Hominisation*, that phase in evolution whereby animal life became transformed into what we now recognise as the species *homo sapiens sapiens*, arrived at our present anatomical structure, including brain size, about 200,000 years ago but the first signs of civilised man occurred about 60,000 years ago, when *homo neanderthalensis* began to bury the dead. There is a cave in the Zagros Mountains of Iraq where there is evidence of a ritual burial. Buried with the corpse are fossilised pollen indicating that flowers had been buried with the man in an orderly way. Prior to that there is no evidence that hominids buried their dead. My surmise is this: that a ritual burial indicates a respect for this member of the clan and an honour of this kind indicates respect for someone who is not just a unit in a clan system but is an individual in his own right. Guy de Maupassant has a short story where a sailor at sea had to have his arm amputated. They brought the arm back to the shore and gave it a ritual burial but it leaves the reader with a strange feeling. One does not give an arm a burial but only an individual person. I think that before what I would call the *burial crisis* each human being was only thought of as a limb of the body; the body being the tribe or clan. Just as the arm has a function in the body so the individual had a function in the tribal body, but something changed at the time of the *burial crisi*—the individual was seen to have a value in himself and not just as a function of a unit. This was the beginning of the huge mutation that took place in the upper/middle palaeolithic period. This mutation did not take place overnight but within a developmental process that began about 70,000 years ago and reached completion about 10,000 years ago. Research has shown that there were areas where hominids were more advanced than in other places but, speaking generally, we can say that before 70,000 years ago the individual was a function in a system whereas 60,000 years later he was also an individual in his own right. The mutation, known as the *upper/middle palaeolithic transition* took therefore about 60,000 years to be fully accomplished.

What I have just stated, though, does not mean that the individual as a unit in the system has disappeared off the face of the earth. In every individual there is a "unit-in-the-system" part and a "someone-of-worth-in-him/herself" part.

What does one quite mean when one says that an individual has a value in his own right? It means that there is something of worth aside from the function he serves in the tribe. The tribal goal is survival and the individual is servant to this purpose. It means that the *upper/middle palaeolithic transition* was a change whereby the instinct for survival was replaced by a desire for the absolute; that elements which had been in the service of survival became ends in themselves; that the individual as a source of action became greater than the actions themselves; that he or she had a value which was greater than the function he or she performed within the tribal unit. One human no longer associated with another just because it was necessary for a joint task outside themselves but rather for the mutual enjoyment of each other. Communication which was a binding force for the sake of survival became an end in itself but this meant that the nature of the communication itself changed. Survival demands a togetherness that glues one thing to another in the way that an arm is joined to the torso. When survival as a goal is reasonably achieved then the very nature of the communication changes. Whereas the communication is driven by an outer demand, the engine of movement is outside the individual, and it is not concerned with the individual but with the group, an individual can die and it matters not but the ultimate disaster is if the group perishes. So with survival as goal there is a group cohesion generated from without, but with the advent of civilisation, heralded by the *upper/middle palaeolithic transition,* communication is generated from within the individual. Communication becomes auto-generated from within instead of moulded from without. Communication from within has the following components: desire and imagery. The imagery is dependent upon events in memory that have an interpersonal significance; in other words the memory-events signify something inner, something invisible. The relation between persons, after the advent of civilisation, is inner to inner rather than outer stuck to outer. Whereas before, one was stuck to another by the binding power of the survival instinct, now another factor comes into play. I have to reach across out of my isolation to the inner world of the other. To do this I have to generate an image which is, at the same time, both a radar signal of the other's inner world, a transmission of a signal to the other, and a manifestation of my own invisible inner life. So the generated image is of a part of my own inner invisible self and also that of the other. It means that part of me and part of the other are one.

This oneness is what I call the absolute. It transcends the two people but at the same time is totally immanent within them. This is prior to the emergence of language. Language has a twofold function: to categorise a range of images of parts and at the same time to particularise and give refined expression to those parts.

I have written as if prior to the *upper/middle palaeolithic transition* there was only the survival instinct in operation and that after it only an exchange relation between persons. The first statement may be largely true but the instinct for survival remains a powerful force subsequent to the advent of civilisation and there remains a conflict between these two motivational principles. The horrors of war which shock us with their appalling massacres are manifestations of the group survival motive; when we are shocked by them our thinking is motivated by the absolute.

* * *

The brain had the capability for this mutation 150,000 years earlier so what was it that happened so dramatically only yesterday, a mere 50,000 years ago? And how did that come about? The first evidence we have of representational art is the lion/man ivory statuette 28 centimetres high from Hohlenstein-Stadel in southern Germany which is between 30,000 and 33,000 years old. Paintings in the Chauvet Cave in the Ardèche in France (discovered only in 1994) date from the same period. Lascaux and Altamira came later—about 20,000 years ago. There are cave paintings in Australia such as the one in Groote Eylandt in the Gulf of Carpentaria that are contemporaneous with Lascaux and Altamira if not older.

Coherent representation and feeling are partners and the one cannot exist without the other. A feature of the psychotic area of the personality is that there is no sensual representation and therefore no feeling. Representation and feeling both ontogenetically and psychogenetically chart a dramatic development in the human entity. Psychogenetically it is as significant as the beginning of bipedalism in the process of *hominisation*. But how did that dramatic mutation took place? How it took place is a mystery. Mithen and other palaeontologists have put forward a thesis which, however, I believe to be faulted. They hold that there are different modules in the mind and that in the *upper/middle palaeolithic transition* a fluidity began to happen between these different modules. This, however, fails, I believe, to describe the essence of what occurred in this fantastic moment in the human story because it was the happening without which civilisation could not have occurred. The question is "What really was the *upper/middle palaeolithic transition?*" The so-called *upper/middle palaeolithic transition* was a momentous event in the unfolding human drama which is obscured by that drab name it has been given. Happily Steven Mithen (1996, pp. 170–210) calls it the "big bang of human culture". What occurred at this peak moment in the human story was that ingredients which until then were a means to an end, now became ends in themselves. The most important of these ends was communication which was now enjoyed for its own sake. This was manifest in dancing, music, painting, sculpture, and friendship. Language developed alongside these different arts. I propose Tolstoy's definition of art in his essay *What is Art?* (1899) in which he dismisses the aesthetic theories of Baumgarten, Kant, Schiller, Fichte, and Schelling who centre their explanation upon an object that gives pleasure, thus placing them in the company of Bentham and Freud who based human motivation on this same principle. Tolstoy instead defines art as a form of communication. Tolstoy's definition carries conviction for me. It also takes art in its essence as constituting a relation between persons rather than a solipsistic phenomenon.

It is when communication becomes an end in itself that representation emerges in the mind. Why? It is that the representation is more important than the thing of which it is a transformation. Because when communication is an end in itself then it becomes the act which requires an inner gathering prior to the act. Representation is that inner gathering before the act of communication occurs. Charlotte Balkanyi has described this in reference to language where she says this:

> Speech and verbalization are not identical concepts. A fraction of a second before producing speech, the speaker verbalizes his thought. In the act of speaking the first step is verbalization, the second is speech. (1964, p. 64)

Verbalisation is the particular representation that refers to communication via language. Language is one form of communication so representation is the superordinate concept of which verbalisation is one of its modes. Representation is the more general "gathering in" state that is preparatory to the act of communication. This communication may be a gesture, a tone of voice, a song, a painting, a sculpture, or speech.

This "gathering in" unifies the personality. Panic, mental illness, trauma, madness all refer to a state of affairs when elements in the personality are in disarray. Healing occurs when these are brought together. Paul Tillich expresses it thus: "Health is not the lack of divergent trends in our bodily or mental or spiritual life, but the power to keep them united. And healing is the act of reuniting them after the disruption of their unity" (1973, p. 52). The supreme exemplar of communication for its own sake is realised in friendship. A friend, as opposed to an ally, is someone I am with for his own sake or her own sake. There is no purpose beyond that. I and the other enjoy each other's company. When my friend dies I do not want to just toss his body on a rubbish dump; I give it a ritual burial instead; I place some flowers by it as a sign of beauty. The value of the person for his or her own sake is expressed clearly by Homer when he describes Achilles's grief at the death of his friend, Patroclus. In a more systematic way Cicero says this in *Laelius: on Friendship* with a stubborn insistence:

> Anyone who wants to allege that a friendship is formed for the sake of advantage seems to me to be doing away with the most attractive things such an association can offer. What we enjoy in a friend is not the profit we derive from him, but the affection. Any practical benefit that goes with this affection only gives satisfaction when it is the product of a warm heart.

Prior to this huge mutation the act of communication was the servant of a subsequent act. When communication became an end in itself then something else emerged. One might, for neatness, want to say that representation is to communication after the "huge mutation" what communication was to survival prior to this evolutionary event, yet this would be incorrect. This is because although in the latter it would be true to say that communication is the servant of species survival it is not true to say that representation is the servant of communication. This is because they are twin realities.

It is that something else emerged with the *upper/middle palaeolithic transition*: intentionality. There is this tripartite interlocking chain of elements that emerged: that communication became an end in itself, representation as the "preparation for action", and intentionality. The thrust for survival is a blind force like those forces that govern the inanimate world. There is no "preparation for action"—the organism is driven. The autonomic nervous system is part of it. So breathing, heart beat, hearing, seeing, touching are part of the thrust for survival. Intentionality means that there is a cause whose source is to be found in the organism. The instincts, like hunger, thirst, and the need for shelter from extremes of heat or cold are also in the service of survival but here, as opposed to the autonomic nervous system, intention is not entirely annihilated. By intention we mean a cause which finds its source within the organism. Someone can decide to starve himself as did those men in the Maze prison in Northern Ireland in recent times. The stimulus-response psychology is based upon the thesis that the thrust for survival is the overarching principle that explains everything so that the organism reacts to the outer stimulus without any possibility of not doing so. It is a psychology, therefore, that would be true for humans before the *upper/middle palaeolithic transition* but not after. So it is a psychological principle that is about 50,000 years out of date. It is out of date if it is described as being the only motivating principle; it is currently applicable if it is recognised as a shared motivational principle. Communication prior to this transition is also a slave to survival. In this system the individuals within the group are under one governing law and therefore are not truly separate. Separation of one from another means that one can and does act differently from another but the thrust for survival joins all in the group into a merged oneness. The herd and the thrust for survival are joint entities: a sensual oneness without separation. Separation occurs on the basis of inner differentiating capacity or, in other words, intentionality. It is only when someone within the herd stands up and says he is prepared *not* to survive that separateness appears on the landscape.

This however is extremely difficult. These joint principle—means becoming ends in themselves, representation and intentionality—that emerged with the *upper/middle palaeolithic transition* are frequently in conflict with the thrust for survival and being merged with the herd. The crowd puts pressure upon the individual to conform to its blind master. There is a strong need in human beings to have substance, to stand on solid ground. This solid ground may be found in two quite distinct place—in the herd or in an unexplained value.

The most frightening experience for someone is to be nowhere; I wake up and find I am in some interplanetary craft adrift in outer space. I look around and planet earth I cannot see but only a few stars in the distance and the craft I am in is heading I know not where and

I have no control of it; it takes me where it wills. I will do anything to be established somewhere; to find solid ground beneath my feet. I look at the trees around me and see their sturdy trunks with roots implanted in the soil deep beneath them. I look for this earth in which I can put down my roots and find that there are two places in which I can plant them: in the herd of which I am a part or planting myself into existence itself. The essence of my own being is that it is *in relation*. It is fashioned in *openness to*. It cannot be to nothing. So it is *in relation* either to the herd or to existence itself of which the herd and myself are a part. In other words I either plant my *openness to* a particular, a part of the whole or to the whole. If I attach myself to the part I am an object, a cog in the wheel; I am an individual but not a person. If I enter into connection with the whole then my being expands; light floods all the parts and I am a person. I am a person to the extent to which I am opened to the whole; I am a mass product to the extent to which I am implanted in the herd *to the exclusion* of the whole. It is this shutting out of the whole which is the source of madness and makes me a non-person. Sleeping with mother and killing father, the Oedipus complex, is the mythical manner of expressing this primordial truth. Freudian theorists have sometimes taken it literally instead of metaphorically. Thought of in this way the Oedipus complex can be activating a whole current of thinking within a culture, not just within the family culture. Polanyi emphasises the way this kind of elimination occurs in a school of think-ing which can dominate a whole academic world:

> A powerful movement of critical thought has been at work to elimi-nate any quest for an understanding that carries with it the meta-physical implications of a groping for reality behind a screen of appearances … Our acknowledgment of understanding as a valid form of knowing will go a long way towards liberating our minds from this violent and inefficient despotism. (1959, pp. 20–21)

Every human being is torn between these two alternatives: either to fasten myself upon the crowd or enter relations with existence itself. The Latin word *entrare* can be used as a technical description of the latter mode of relating. Someone will be pressured by the herd to the extent to which she is fastened to it. She will be less pressured to the extent to which she has directed herself *in relationship* to the whole of existence. Someone may be the target of mockery, hate, injustice, or vengeance and may be able to bear that, if she is in relation to existence itself. The influence of the crowd upon the individual is vividly described by George Orwell in his essay *Shooting an Elephant* (1957). An elephant had gone "must" in the bazaar of a small town in Burma. This is a temporary madness which envelops the animal and which passes off after a few hours. Orwell, as police commissioner, had been called by the local policeman to deal with this elephant which had ravaged stalls in a bazaar and trampled a man to death. Orwell arrived to see the animal in a paddy field at the edge of the village. He knew that he had to watch and see if the animal's "must" had passed off. So, with gun in hand, he watched but behind him were two thousand natives waiting for him to shoot the elephant. He glanced around and saw all the expectant eyes. He observed that the "must" had passed off and so knew that he did not need to shoot but the power of the group expectation was too overwhelming so he shot the animal. He writes poignantly:

> I glanced round at the crowd that had followed me. It was an immense crowd, two thousand at the least and growing every minute. It blocked the road for a long distance on either side. I looked at the sea of yellow faces above the garish clothes—faces all happy and excited over this bit of fun, all certain that the elephant was going to be shot. They were watching me as they would watch a conjurer about to perform a trick. They did not like me, but with the magical rifle in my hands I was momentarily worth watching. And suddenly I realized that I should have to shoot the elephant after all. The people expected it of me and I had got to do it; I could feel their two thousand wills pressing me forward, irresistibly. (p. 95)

Then he ends his essay by admitting,

> … afterwards I was very glad that the coolie had been killed; it put me legally in the right and it gave me a sufficient pretext for shooting the elephant. I often wondered whether any of the others grasped that I had done it solely to avoid looking a fool. (pp. 91–99)

It is surviving as a figure of respect that becomes all-important. It is the pressure of the "unit-in-the-system" that became dominant for

Orwell but the "someone-of-worth-in-himself" was active enough not to blind him to the force of the "unit-in-the-system" for if it had been he would not have been aware of his motive for shooting the elephant. To be laughed at rubs out one's substance to the extent to which it is fastened onto the herd for its self-esteem. The fact that George Orwell could be so candid about his motive implies that he himself was very largely connected to existence itself. I think one can posit that when he decided to resign from being an Indian police commissioner he was then in the mode of *entrare* to a staggering degree. It is what has made him so rightly famous.

What emerged also at the *upper/middle palaeolithic transition* was a unity of elements that made up the fact of communication.

We are conscious of things done to us through our feelings but to become aware of what we ourselves emotionally do to others requires something greater than us to reflect it to us. The only way it can grasp its own active source is to focus upon an object that transcends itself and yet includes itself. The only object that fulfils this objective is not, strictly speaking, an object because "object" suggests something particular, something that of its nature must exclude, and this will mean that the active source which we are trying to grasp must necessarily be excluded. I say necessarily because the subject which we are trying to grasp is other than the object and so cannot be embraced by it. The act of comprehension must be total enough to embrace not just one object but all objects and here "all objects" includes the subjective self as an object. So a word is needed that points to a reality that is capable of including both the object and the subject. I propose the phrase "all-inclusive principle". This is internal and external and of an undifferentiated nature.

The act of comprehension that mirrors the "all-inclusive principle" is pure subjectivity. This is because this act is creative. Pure subjectivity is the creative, shorn of all uncreated elements. Through this creative principle the subject is transformed into the "all-inclusive principle" through which it is able to grasp hold of itself. There is nothing outside it. Yet because we do not know it directly but through this "all-inclusive principle", we experience it as coming from outside.

The creative is what is most truly me. I can only call *mine* that which I create. With money I can buy a painting and call it mine. However, it is not truly mine until I have interpreted it from my own inner experience. So what do I mean by "truly"? The purchase of a painting is an external act. It has moved from one location to another. An interpretation, however, is an internal act that embraces the object and transforms it. Because the interpretation is all-inclusive the source and the object have undergone a transformation.

I am making here the creative principle synonymous with the ego. This is different from Freud's definition of the ego which processes the sense impressions from the external and internal world. Freud defines the ego as a surface phenomenon. For him it is on the surface of the personality and then deepened through identifications but the source of the personality lies in an instinctual deposit. *Triebe*, drives, have no subjectivity; they are blind forces. Sublimation means that the instinctual discharge is turned into a socially useful factor. The agent responsible for this is the creative principle. Freud describes the phenomenon of sublimation but not the inner agent responsible for it. For Freud the drives are the governing factor in the personality; for me it is the creative principle which needs to defer to the thrust for survival but is ultimately its master. These two principles are inside us and often in conflict. The example of George Orwell faced with whether he should shoot the elephant or not is a good example. The all-inclusive principle invited him not to shoot the elephant but the need to fulfil the expectations of the group dictated otherwise. His survival as a group member reigned victorious over his own wish not to shoot the elephant.

Someone can be governed by the drives or by the creative principle. There is a struggle between these two within the personality. Tolstoy elaborates this struggle in many of his writings. The following passage from *War and Peace* describes it well:

> It was past one o'clock when Pierre left his friend. It was a luminous Petersburg midsummer night. Pierre took an open cab intending to drive straight home. But the nearer he got to the house the less he felt like sleep on such a night, which was more like evening or early morning. It was light enough to see far down the empty streets. On the way Pierre remembered that the usual set were to meet for cards at Anatole Kuragin's that evening, after which there was generally a drinking bout, finishing off with one of Pierre's favourite pastimes.
>
> "It would be nice to go to Kuragin's," he thought, but immediately recalled his promise to Prince Andrei not to go there again. Then, as happens to people with no strength of character, such a passionate desire came over him for one last taste of the familiar

dissipation that he decided to go. And the thought immediately occurred to him that his word to Prince Andrei was not binding because before he had given it he had already promised Prince Anatole to come. "Besides," he reasoned, "all these *words of honour* are mere convention and have no precise significance, especially if one considers that by to-morrow one may be dead, or some extraordinary accident may happen to sweep away all distinctions between honour and dishonour." Arguments of this kind often occurred to Pierre, nullifying all his resolutions and intentions. He went to Kuragin's. (1869, pp. 33–34)

This creative principle is also unifying. The facts in the personality are not linked to one another. The creative principle transforms them into a oneness. This is only possible because this creative principle is at the same time both transcendent and immanent. It is only capable of transforming sensations coming from within and without because it transcends them as a category and also is totally immanent in them. Hence the all-inclusive principle. This is in tune with Schopenhauer for whom the *noumenon* is not an unknown as Kant taught but rather an inner subjective principle. If the principle of unity arises from the "unit-in-the-system" then there is an Oedipal exclusion; if from the "someone-of-worth-in-himself" then this is governed by the all-inclusive principle and there is no exclusion.

It is a creative action which moulds itself according to the sense impressions, considering these sense impressions as a medium.

CHAPTER THREE

Manifestations of the creative principle

The percept is a manifestation of the creative principle of which *representation* is the same element but now embodied within thought. This is when something is produced that has an objective presence but because it is embraced within a thought process it now has a subjective element that suffuses it. This subjective side of *representation* is captured by the term *realisation*. So, for instance, I am reading Tolstoy's *Anna Karenina* and reach the point where Anna is giving birth to the baby which she conceived out of wedlock with Vronsky. Here is a psychological fact being represented; it is a fact but it arises through Tolstoy's own experience embodied in an act of understanding. Tolstoy represents a personal experience in this statement. The reader might pass over the statement giving it no significance or it might also generate a realisation within the reader. If the reader, in the moment of reading Tolstoy's statement, has a similar realisation then a living communication has occurred between Tolstoy and the reader. Although separated in time and place, Tolstoy and the reader are together in that moment. It is a communication between persons. Physical death does not destroy this if there is a written communication which then evokes the realisation in the reader. Tolstoy's essence lives on; the body is dead but the person is alive. An element in the person then is outside space and time. *Realisation* is the communication between persons. Language is the signal that points to it.

The creative principle is manifest in a produced object. It can never be isolated from it. *Realisation* as the subjective aspect of *representation* is thus produced by the creative principle formed between persons. *Representation* is also produced by the creative principle but it becomes a realisation when it sets fire within the hearts of two persons. In fact *representation* and *realisation* are one thing but the former can exist without the latter when there is no receptive person set on fire by it. When the object and the subject are seen from the perspective of a reality of which these two are one then *representation* and *realisation* are both present. *Realisation* is the registration of oneness; *representation* is founded on two-ness. The latter arises from a failure to reflect on the unity of being.

The second manifestation is *understanding.* The act of *understanding* itself is wordless. A fact or series of facts are transformed through the creative principle into an act of *understanding*. This *understanding* suffuses the objects which are all then *informed* by the "all-inclusive principle". In the way that volume suffuses the elements of which it is attributed so also does *understanding* do so of the objects within its compass. In the quote from Tolstoy there is an act of *understanding* of which the statement "it was not until he saw his dying wife that he knew his own heart" is a manifestation. The difference between *realisation* and *understanding* is that the former registers the oneness whereas an act of *understanding* has a limited focus. If, for instance, it relates to the way a symbol represents an invisible emotion this focus inevitably shuts out other elements in the mental landscape such as shame or guilt.

This *matching* of a word or words to that understanding is the third manifestation. The *understanding* here needs to be the governor otherwise the *understanding* is crushed by the word. The word needs to be the servant to the act of *understanding*. Effort and practice is needed to effect good *matching*.

Understanding is a psychic act but it needs an instrument to bring it about. There is the subject and there is a something out there. The subject and the something-out-there are brought into connection with each other in the act of understanding. It is a great relief when someone is understood by another. The two share a togetherness. When someone understands me I am no longer in isolation. But the subject needs an instrument to bring about this togetherness, to fashion an act of understanding. This instrument is something which exists but in such a way that it is immanent in both the subject and the object. It is an art work. There is an event which frightened me and I want to explain to someone why it frightened me. I will recount an incident to try to elucidate it. A young girl of thirteen went to a seaside resort with her parents. She was playing on the beach making a sandcastle while her parents went swimming in the sea. There was an undertow and her mother and father were carried out to sea and were unable to get back to the shore and they were struggling in the water in a state of desperation. The lifeguards saw them and went out in a lifeboat and pulled the two of them into the boat and brought them back to shore. They placed them on the sand and set about giving them the kiss of life. A ring of people surrounded the immobile bodies and their little thirteen-year-old daughter joined them. As she was standing there looking at her inert parents she heard one of the people say, "They're dead." Now, fortunately as it happened, the lifeguards managed to revive them and they lived. A week later the young teenager was back at school but in a rebellious state. She did not do her homework, did not pay attention in class so she was sent to see a psychotherapist who happened to be me. She told me the incident that I have just described and, although I felt sorry for her and realised how upsetting it was I had not understood. Then she told me again and I suddenly realised that when she heard the man saying, "They're dead", her parents had died; she suffered the shock of their death. She said to me "And when I got back to school everyone acted as if nothing had happened." At that moment I realised with shock that she had undergone the death of her parents without any support. If her parents had physically died then friends and relatives would have gathered around her in support but this death, which was a real death for her, was unseen so she was left on her own with it. Now how was it that I suddenly understood? I saw her standing on the sand—and I can still see her—among a ring of strangers looking at the inert bodies of her parents and hearing someone saying "They're dead". What was it that gave me that act of understanding? It was the image of her standing watching her dead parents, standing there uncomforted among strangers. At that moment I was a young teenager watching my parents like corpses on the beach with someone saying "They're dead". I think the central image was of being alone with my parents, on whom I had totally relied, suddenly dead in front of me. The image of my parents driving away, leaving me in a boarding school in another country and a thousand miles from home and me being left among teachers and boys who were all strangers came to me. When she told me a second time the image of my own experience was the instrument that enabled the act of understanding.

It is important to differentiate between my sorrow for her when she first told me and my act of understanding when she told me the second time. In the first case I was an outsider, like one of those strangers. In the second case I was in a shared experience with her. My own experience was the instrument through which the act of understanding occurred. Now I did not have a conscious image of my own loss of my parents at the age of eleven when they disappeared down the drive in that hearse-like motor-car, but on the second occasion when she told me I believe that this emotional memory was the instrument that fashioned understanding. She was no longer alone any more than I was. She needed me not as a stranger but as a fellow sufferer. I believe that I also was wrested from isolation in that moment. I was sharing an emotional memory. I did not share it with her in the way she shared hers with me but I believe that in that sudden moment of shock when I felt close to tears at the shocking awfulness of what had happened to her that she felt me as a fellow sufferer. There is communication at this level before there are any words. The act of understanding happens in a flash, in a nanosecond. Images followed by words are the elaboration of that happening.

So what I want to emphasise here is the image born of experience that is necessary for the act of understanding. The outer details are always different but the inner experience is similar enough for the connection to occur. I did not have the experience of believing that my parents were dead but I did have the experience of losing them while on my own and among strangers and although her experience was worse I think there was enough similarity for the connection to occur. She and I were also at about the same age when the events occurred. The mediaeval theologian and philosopher Meister Eckhart wrote: "… if you are unlike the truth of which we want to speak, you cannot understand me" (1981, p. 199).

The instrument which enables the act of understanding is an experience of similarity. The instrument which enables the act of understanding is an experience which is in sympathy with the experience of the other. The Russian philosopher and mystic, Vladimir Solovyov, referred to this as "harmony of the similar" (1918, p. 68) and he stresses that it is not that the two are thrust into a sameness with each other, or an identification of one with the other but that they are different, rather that there is some shared event which, though different, is similar enough to allow a spark of connection to occur. In order to understand the particular distress of the other I reach for a parallel within my own experience. I then use that to enter the experience of the other. In the moment of understanding I and the other are oned through togetherness achieved through the mutuality of experience. Because the experience is similar it enters the experience of the other. But it only becomes such an instrument when it is shorn of the outer particulars. That moment when I lost my parents—a loss of those I loved and utterly depended upon—was a trauma. Reaching to this loss and arriving at it brought me into sympathetic union with the young woman who thought her parents were dead. We were together. The intensity of the inner experience shut out all those differences between us—I was an adult man of forty years of age; she a young woman of thirteen. My experience had been of losing my parents on my first day of boarding school; hers was losing her parents on a beach. In the act of understanding, in that momentary flash, my experience and hers are in a joint intensity and all the outer contours of our lives are shut out or, to use the structure formulated by Polanyi, the out-works of our lives are subsidiary to this focal point. The focal point being the union.

Now to generalise. The action is an entering into the experience of the other; the instrument through which this is achieved is a parallel experience, again shorn of all its subsidiary elements. So in the example given: me seeing my parents leaving me at boarding school when I was aged eleven is subsidiary to the focal point of an experience of loss of people to whom I was closely attached. We can therefore consider that there are a series of focal experiences common to all human beings and that these function as the instruments to bring about an entry into the other's experience. It is therefore an entry through one's own inner experience.

There is a correlate here which is worth dwelling upon. It is that entry into one's own experience sometimes requires the shock of another's trauma to unlock the gateway to it. Clinicians speak of a patient "getting through" to the therapist. The experience of the other has this force behind it. There is an implication here that there is a barrier in all of us against this act of *entrare*. Why is this so? In order to answer this, it is necessary to understand more fully what has been stated above. Although I have used my own experience of "losing" my parents when I first went to boarding school as the instrument through which I understood the trauma my patient suffered when her parents "died", yet this is not the whole story because another aspect of my understanding was that the "death" of her parents was unrecognised by others, and I understood that she had thereby suffered the death of her parents alone and that it was being on her own in the disaster she had suffered which was so traumatic and it was that which I understood when she told me the second time. Now I also had an experience in my early adulthood where, like Hamlet, I had a knowledge of something which I was unable to share. But I would not want to claim that it was these experiences in themselves alone which were the instruments through which the act of understanding took place, but rather that they were "screen memories" for something more basic and more painful. It was Freud who coined the term "screen memory" and by it he meant that a memory in adulthood or childhood is poignant because it hides a more fundamental memory or experience. Therefore I think that the conjunction of these two experiences of mine: losing my parents when I was aged eleven and suffering an experience in loneliness in early adulthood, were "screen memories" for something more primitive and more universal. I think that Freud's "screen memory" does not so much conceal a memory but rather a universal experience—a painful one that all human beings have passed through. One is the death of the one I love and depend upon, and the other is knowledge in loneliness, and these are universals in that everyone has experienced them and they have subsequently become "screened" behind more adult memories. So now I return to my question: why is there this barrier against these universal experiences? It is because awareness of them puts a demand upon me: that I open myself to a basic human-ness shared by all; that I open myself to this is-ness. It also means renouncing a surface belonging in favour of this deeper reality. To belong is a basic human need. I belong to my family but ultimately there is a deeper belonging and it is this which has a prior claim upon me. Death spells the end of this individual life but the world still exists. It is this existence which has the prior claim. Why is this so difficult? Why do I put so great a weight behind my own individual existence? What I am saying here is not that relations with my family and friends will ever be less important than relations with "strangers" but that the deeper claim that I am talking of only occurs when there has first been a death of an attachment which is surface to surface; it is when this has died that the deeper claim asserts its primacy. There is a fear that if I let go of this surface attachment to my own individual existence I will plunge into nothingness. Out of this fear I cling to my own individual existence and its surface attachment. When psychiatrists, psychologists, or psychotherapists talk of someone thinking "concretely" they are referring to this elemental fear of nothingness which makes me cling desperately to something solid and physical. To understand concreteness we have to see that it constitutes a flight from an abyss of emptiness.

These universals are there in the personality but we are required to appropriate them personally so they become ours. The memories that screen them give us entry into the universal so the screen is also a personal revealer. It gives us a personal entry—*entrare*—into the universal. This entry which is unique to me makes the universal a personal possession and brings me into brotherhood with my fellow human beings. It also transforms the surface to surface attachment to family members in such a way that the relation is inner to inner which allows freedom between myself and my parents, wife, or children.

So these "screen memories" are important signals requiring my attention. They are there in memory in order to open me to these universals of human experience. They are the registrations within my own individual person of these universals. They are therefore not abstract but enfleshed into the current of my own life. Therefore although they are universals the particular experience of them will be different for Philippa, for Joseph, or for someone who lived long ago in a different age and culture. Therefore they are universal and yet uniquely personal. This universal is only meaningful when it is filtered through the lens of my own experience.

Now there is a substitute instrument which looks like understanding but is not. Instead of generating an image out of my own memory-bank I summon an instrument which belongs to someone else. It may be an image that was fine for Darwin, for Freud, for Karl Marx, for Heinz Kohut, Melanie Klein, Wilfred Bion, Donald Winnicott, Frances Tustin, or Ronald Fairbairn, but does not apply to me. The universal becomes a meaningless abstraction when it is filtered through someone else's lens unless there is a bond of sympathy between me and this other figure. What I mean here is if the figure whose lens I am looking through is giving expression to something that adequately frames my experience then it is fine but not if this is not the case. What is certain is that the whole range of thought of a particular clinician can never be fully faithful to my own experience. If that were the case then that other person would be me. So unless this figure gives a particular and adequate expression of my own experience it will be foreign to me and will not be the right instrument for my own act of understanding: it is not my own construction and therefore is not me but something outside me. If the theoretical explanation has been expounded by someone because it is an expression of his own experience and that is one that is shared by me in the same way as I had a shared experience with that young teenage girl then it will be genuine and known to be so by my patient, but if this is not the case then my own personhood will have been buried inside the corpse of my instrumental figure. There has been no *entrare* in its fashioning. Within the social sciences there is a vast storehouse of such instruments and it is easy for me to go to one of them to fashion my act of understanding, but it always remains a pale colourless act which deceives both me and the other unless it expresses my own experience. It is the way in which one word, phrase, or sentence may express my experience accurately whereas another, which is a close semantic relative, does not. If what I borrow from the social science storehouse does not correspond to my inner essential experience it will be meaningless. In such a case myself and the other remain in isolation from each other.

The reason why we frequently grab as our instrument something which is alien to our experience is that there is in us a deep hatred of experience, as Wilfred Bion emphasised: "There is a hatred of having to learn by experience at all, and lack of faith in the worth of such a kind of learning" (1968, p. 89). He also says in this same paragraph that it boils down to a hatred of a process of development. When it is personal experience it is painful but it also puts a demand upon me to open my mind to that deeper experience of the universal in the light of which I see the tragic in the details of my life. Events from the past float into my mind which envelop me in shame; I assent to passions inside me here and now which betray the truth; I hide from the hard path ahead of me and put a veil of illusion around it.

The generation of a memory or an image is always painful or disturbing. It puts demands upon me now today, although it may issue from a memory of long ago. Even though the person or persons involved in the memory may be dead, yet the memory and its generation demand a change of emotional direction in myself. I can avoid this by going to a "system" explanation that is devoid of life-challenge. When I read something which "clicks" it is because there is a togetherness between the event being described and a similar one in my own life. Again it is not the outer clothing of the event which makes it "click" for me but the inner content of it—the universal which has been filtered through a lens which resonates with my experience. So in the case I have quoted it is the inner loss of my parents that brings me together with the inner loss of the parents of my teenage patient. The inner emotional happenings that have a startling array of different clothes. Those inner emotional happenings can probably be summarised into loss of a loved one, disappointment through collapse of an ideal, shame at my own inadequacy, guilt over my own destruction of human-ness, and apprehension of the tragedy consequent upon human ignorance. It is only too understandable that we avoid these disasters of the soul within. They are shockingly painful and wear down the human spirit. It is when we avoid these that we go to an explanation that is outside our own painful pilgrimage. Now, as I have just suggested, we might go to an explanation generated by a psychologist, a psychoanalyst, or a philosopher, and if there is an inner sympathy between that thinker and myself then his explanatory principle will be personal to me. The two persons of myself and that particular thinker will be together sharing an experience. So, for instance, I turn to Melanie Klein because she believes that human beings construct their world from their earliest childhood and that "clicks" for me, but her invocation of the death instinct and the infant's fear of annihilation through fear of it is, I am sure, wrong; so also Freud's idea of a screen memory "clicks" for me while his view that love is like a reservoir which must not be used wastefully shocks my sensibilities to the core; Michael Balint's view that there is an undeveloped function of the personality originating through some misalliance between mother and baby seems right to me but his underlying determinism seems wrong. I do see what Melanie Klein means in her invocation of the death instinct and I see what Michael Balint means but this is another matter. It is like seeing why people laugh at a joke but not finding it funny myself. If I run to an explanation which does not correspond with my inner experience, rather than make the effort to generate an image which does bring about a communion of spirits, then it is an empty vessel. It has no soul. It is the same principle by which we make the effort to select a word or phrase that fits the experience rather than subdue the experience to a word. This is where language can be misused. It is easier to submit to a word and crush the experience than to find the word or words that correspond closely to the event or aspiration which is seeking expression. Words are our servants but we are forever turning them into our masters. Before there is thinking with words there is thinking with images. These images which are auto-generated or produced by the inner creative spirit are tuned to the emotions and produced by the emotions. The words we use are required to match these images. Such words which are best described as poetic need to be differentiated from words which are used to categorise a series of subjects. So, for instance, red hot fury might describe a momentary flash of anger whereas "aggressive drives" might be a suitable heading for a folder in a filing cabinet containing a whole package of different images of which "flash of anger" might be one. The same principle applies to a theoretical system whether it be of Freud, Melanie Klein, or Michael Balint. In such a system there is an agglomeration of images which are only loosely connected. Sometimes their connection is just that they were put forth by the same author, but no author enjoys total consistency in his or her thinking.

Every seminal thinker has a history of development and usually there is a growth in consistency so ideally at the end of the person's life there is a consistent pattern governing all they have written but this utopian ideal is never achieved. Some thinkers die young and had they lived longer would have recast their theories. Those who live to be eighty or ninety would certainly change what they had formulated at that age if they were to live to the age of Methuselah. Therefore the thinking of great geniuses like Newton, Darwin, Freud, or Marx are always inconsistent and hencethe acceptance of the whole package of their thinking indicates that the disciple has annihilated his or her thinking capacity in submission to the hero.

In the thinking of any innovative clinician there is a mixture of personal insights and borrowed concepts. Usually a clinician starts with a system which is entirely, or almost entirely, a pre-existing one into which he is inserted; then slowly he begins to develop a language and a theory which matches his inner personal imagery but he never entirely lets go of the theory into which he was first born. Therefore the theory that goes under the name of a person is always an agglomeration. It is a mixture of personal insight and borrowed theory. It is like the difference in physics between a rock which is made up of many different chemical substances and therefore an agglomeration and sulphuric acid which has a single coherent structure.

What needs more exploration is why it is that what match the emotions are these visual images, this poetic language and not the language of categorisation. If I turn to someone and say "I love you" it evokes a response. Colours and music carry with them a similar demand, They tune into fear, love, or hatred; I cannot remain neutral. Scarlet or a blow on a trumpet violate my drowsy complacency; they break into my world, they intrude into it, my passions are aroused. They wake me up. My sleep is interrupted. Red carries with it rage, fury, alarm, excitement, but the inadequacy of words hits one here. These words I have just written down do not convey the primitiveness of red. An artist cannot say it in words and it is because this is so, he has to say it with paints. Colours, together with music, represent the emotions more closely than words. The word "red" is a pale sign of the vibrant colour. Colours and musical tones are what Locke referred to as "secondary qualities". Primary qualities are extension, density, and volume. Because the latter are measurable and the same whoever the viewer happens to be, they have become the darlings of the scientific world; they belong to the group, to the institution. Science has become twinned to the institution, the corporation, or social organisation. There is no difference between you and me in this; we are both units in a system so that the focus is upon the system of which we are both parts. There is a red table in the room. Two people take out a ruler and measure it; it is two feet long, one foot wide, and two inches thick, and the legs are each a foot long. These are facts and if I come along and say, that table is three feet long, I can be shown to be wrong. If I say that I love that table, no one can say I am wrong; my friend says that he hates it. Why? Its redness is vulgar and intrusive; but I love it. I love violent landscapes, tropical storms, and rough seas, but my friend likes gentle green pastures, temperate climate, and the calm waters of a lagoon. Because secondary qualities are capable of being registered differently by each person they have been dismissed by scientists. Damasio says that when he first started working with feelings he was disparaged:

> When I started musing about how the brain managed to create the mind, I accepted the established advice that feelings were out of the scientific picture … It took me awhile to see the degree to which the injunction was unjustified and to realize that the neurobiology of feelings was no less viable than the neurobiology of vision or memory. (2003, pp. 4–5)

I believe this disparagement is because we are talking of the secondary qualities through which the individual person is designated. These secondary qualities are contemptuously referred to as "subjective"—i.e., not to be relied upon. Because I, Neville, see something differently from John it is disparaged. This means the difference between one individual and another is thus dismissed. What are endorsed are those qualities which are the same for all. So the language of categorisation is that of sameness but inherent in emotions is difference. Emotions are the communication between two individuals but where there is no difference no communication exists; there is no need for it. We are constituted of two parts—sameness and difference. The language of categorisation expresses the sameness; colour, music, and poetry are rooted in difference and are the communicative medium between different beings.

So I have stressed above the similarity that existed between the experience of the young thirteen-year-old girl and my own when I was at a similar age, and I said that I thought behind both events was a universal experience of death, of loss. But, the two events were not the same. To use the word "identity" for the two would be incorrect. She and I were different. Her trauma was different from mine but there was, as I have quoted from Solovyov, a *harmony of the similar*—a similarity which respected the difference between us.

CHAPTER FOUR

The creative principle generates the person

The creative principle has the function of transforming the "givens" in the personality. These "givens" are the drives, inner elements, and outer stimuli. One needs to think of them as dry seeds which lie inert in the personality, dead and inactive until water and sunlight has penetrated them. Are these inert substances the same as what Bion referred to as *beta elements*? I think this is what they are when considered as a generalised category but I suspect that there is a difference between them because they become transformed into a series of discrete though connected psychological functions. One needs to examine in minute detail the functions, name the function and then give a name to the inert seed. To think of it in Bion's terminology we need to consider that there are different sorts of *beta elements* and each sort has the capacity to grow into a different function. Until a transformation has occurred these inner elements and outer stimuli react upon one another in the way in which inanimate pieces of matter react upon each other. Transformed they become functions in the personality. "Function" means that the element serves a purpose within the personality. So one can think that prior to transformation it was there, disconnected to other factors in the personality, but one aspect of the transformation now is a part within a structure. Take a watch to bits and each part lies there inert on the watchmaker's bench but when every part is put together in the correct relation to the others each has a function. So one aspect of transformation is bringing parts in relation to one another and made part of the whole. Its function then can only be understood in relation to the entire structure. The structure's goal will enlighten and define the function.

I want here to distinguish what I am saying here from Ferro's formulation of *alpha elements*. He refers (2005, p. 3) to lumps of *beta elements* that are formed, he says, as a defence mechanism. I believe this is the wrong way of formulating it. This suggests that there is a mechanism that generates *beta elements* but I believe this to be wrong. *Beta elements* are not formed. They are, as it were, raw data waiting to be transformed. But what Ferro may be trying to formulate is the differentiation between *beta elements*—that they are not homogenous.

Whereas before transformation the elements were inert and dead, now they become digested and transformed into a subjective function. I have introduced the term "subjective" which needs defining. Subjective is the word we use to say something is part of *I* or *me*. The *I/me* comes into being through communication. Communication between what? We need to think of it on different levels. There is first communication between the different elements within the personality; between the seeds. Then there is communication between two individuals. Two individuals can coexist next to each other and not be in relation, like two stones lying alongside each other, or they can be in relation to one another. Now when we say "in relation to one another" we mean that there is an opening of the inner of one to the inner of the other. It is not just a geographical proximity. Two human beings can be standing two metres apart from each other or they might be touching, skin to skin. But they can also be open to one another *from within*. Vygotsky, in his scheme for development of mental faculties, says that until adolescence the individual relates one thing to another "according to phenomenal similarity" (1975, pp. 79–80)—things are related according to their surface similarity. So, for instance, two objects that are both blue will be categorised in the same way but at adolescence the blue object might be joined with a brown one because one is a DVD of a film and the other is a videotape of a film. The adolescent puts more weight on the inner content rather than the similarity of colour on the outside. I remember when our elder son was three years old he said one day, "A phone and a stone are similar, Dad, aren't they?" The sounds were similar. He needed to reach adolescence to release him from their surface similarity and bring him into their inner sense. It is this openness from within that brings about the birth of the *I/me*. This within-ness then suffuses the whole personality. Dilthey emphasises this: "The pinnacle of human development is attained when the inwardness of the individual guides and shapes his perceptions and controls his actions at every moment" (1989, pp. 287–288). Penetration into the inner is what characterises the personal as opposed to the individual whose relation to the other is through "phenomenal exteriors".

There is the communication between parts within the individual and also between him and the inwardness of his companion. The inner relation of the one to the other at the individual level is what waters the seeds in each. There is, though, a further element that needs to be brought in that raises the relations between two persons to a level that transcends the two, and this is the reality of which the two are constituted.

This introduces another important dimension. This very way in which I have been expressing myself suggests that there are different parts of the personality, and if, for instance, someone believes he is worthless it is because one undeveloped part is poisoning, as it were, the rest of the personality and there is an interconnection between parts that is injurious to the personality. Parts within are connected, or may be connected, in that same phenomenal way inwardly as they are outwardly or, to put it in more familiar language, the way parts are connected intrapsychically is similar to the way they are connected interpersonally. A sign that they are connected at this phenomenal level is when someone has a bad image of themselves. This is because one part is poisoning the rest of the personality and this is because of the way in which the parts within are connected to each other. I want to look at the way the parts are connected when there is a poison from one part affecting the rest. What sort of connection is occurring here? On what basis is the wholeness of personality achieved? I think the image that is most helpful is that of darkness and light. What I have been suggesting is that as soon as light is poured upon the inner personality then a protective barrier and a caring mother surround the emotional infant—the foetal function one might call it—is looking for development. It seems that the light *is* a caring mother. It seems further that when there is this tender light that this part of the personality no longer secretes a poison into the rest of the personality. It is that the light itself functions as a unifier. The reason for this is that if the inner connection is glue-like, this same hatred which operates in the interpersonal sphere also operates here.

Hatred is a word which, when applied to primitive action, represents a violent discharge. The violent discharge occurring in even one part in the personality contaminates then the whole personality. A cancer has overtaken the whole personality organism.

When this warm light shines upon this handicapped child within, it functions as a nurturing mother. It is nurture that changes the action within from hatred to love. This means then that its relation to other parts of the personality is no longer of an outer to outer, glue-like attachment but inner to inner. What distinguishes love from hatred is that the former finds its centre in a reality which is both in itself but also outside itself whereas hatred is centred upon an outer object that frustrates. It frustrates because there is an underlying desire which produces hatred. The underlying desire is to be something which I am not. I am not content with what I am, with who I am. This desire to be what I am not dislocates all the parts of my personality. To be who I am requires an act—a desire to be who I am. My inner being is *in-relation* and therefore not subject to frustration, not subject to hatred. This *in-relation* is the essence of my being. The desire to be what I am not is to desire to be in isolation, to not be *in* relation. This desire to be not in relation equals a hatred of what I am. Such hatred therefore leaves the personality in an array of unrelated bits.

This desire to be who I am and who I am is *in-relation* which is true of the whole of me but also of each of the parts. The *I* is the *in-relation* of all. If the *I* desires not to be *in-relation* to one part it is because there is an opposition which can only occur if the *I* is made out of the material of "sensation". If on the other hand the *I* is made of the same "stuff" as volume, weight, or density, then there is no opposition between the *I* and the parts because the *I* is *in* the parts in the same way in which volume is in all the parts which constitute it. The *I* is the *in-relation* of all parts just as volume is in all of them.

The "should" arises when the *I* is not so constituted. I think this occurs when there is one part which is undeveloped. Undeveloped means that it is not constituted *in-relation*. This is where the whole affects the part; where the mother functions as the creator of the *in-relation* in the child. Suttie's statement finds its relevance here:

> I saw the possibility that the biological need for nurture might
> be psychologically presented in the infant mind, not as a bun-
> dle of practical organic necessities and potential privations, but

as a pleasure in responsive companionship and as a correlative discomfort in loneliness and isolation. The Freudian conception of self-expression as a "detensioning" process or emotional evacuation now seemed to me to be false and in its place I imagined expression as an offering or stimulus directed to the other person, designed to elicit a response while love itself was essentially a state of active harmonious interplay. (1939, p. 4)

It differs fundamentally from psycho-analysis in introducing the conception of an innate need-for-companionship which is the infant's only way of self-preservation. This need, giving rise to parental and fellowship "love", I put in the place of the Freudian Libido, and regard it as genetically independent of genital appetite. The application of this conception seems to re-orient the whole psycho-analytic dynamics ... (1939, p. 6).

Studies in infant research support what this innovator said over seventy years ago.

We have to look at why a particular part may not be *in-relation* to the others. Why does the *I* disown this part? Not want to enter into relation with it? The easy answer is to say that the *I* is ashamed of this part, but why? The part of which the *I* is ashamed has in it an element that is also true of the *I*. For a link between the *I* and the part to be *inner* there has to be in essence a like to like or similarity to similarity. It is human nature to be on a journey towards; we are in a state of becoming. In this sense we are not adult, never adult. We are *in-relation* to an ultimate end. The undeveloped part is clamouring for the *I* which instantiates the other parts to be where this undeveloped part is; it is like a child clamouring for a mother to attend to her child.

This handicapped child then demands that the *I* recognise its own handicapped nature. It has been said that the agony that many patients come to analysis for today is a cry from the heart, "Who am I?" Underlying this *cri de coeur* is a knowledge of there being an unfashioned *I* but this knowledge is hidden from the *I*.

Shame has dictated a cover-up. Because of *shame* all the rest of the personality has become host to this one part. And a reason for this is supplied by the same Russian thinker Solovyov who has already been mentioned (see Chapter Two, p. 4): it is that there is *shame* when there is not a unity within the personality. But this implies that there is a knowledge that tells me that human life is a unity—a unity that needs to be created. *Shame* is because I am not a unity, because I am stunted in my growth. In Freud's formulation I am *fixated* at a particular point. In *shame* I hide my disunited state. All my energy goes into hiding my disunity. *Shame*, in mythology, is because of sex. In the Biblical account of Adam and Eve they were, after their disgrace, *ashamed* and sought clothes to cover their nakedness. Why is the sexual the focus of this *shame*? It is, I believe, because sexual passion pulls me away from myself. I am together and in one piece and suddenly a sexually attractive woman passes before my field of vision and I am pulled towards her, torn away from myself. But, and this is the most important part, although sexual passion does pull, or is capable of pulling me away from intentional goals, yet one of the greatest mistakes is to take this concretely. I need to explain what I mean here. It does not mean that sexual passion cannot pull me away from myself but that this is a crude instance easily identifiable and therefore stands as a *symbol* for forces that are less easy to detect.

Now the question is: what does the sexual urge therefore symbolise? I think it is an attachment of one thing to another that is blind. An untransformed attachment. In Bion's formulation it is an attachment that has not been worked upon by *alpha function*. They are attached to one another through a magnetism, a gravitational force. It is blind, it is darkness. Light, on the other hand, joins one thing to another through a principle that is internal to the different parts. Ultimately it is through the being of each and in each that the different parts find their coherence. They cohere out of an inner harmony that is rooted in a reality which Solovyov refers to a "harmony of the similar" (1918, p. 68). This harmony that he talks about arises from the totality in which all living things participate.

This means that what Solovyov refers to as the "harmony of the similar" finds its similarity in the togetherness in truth of both participants. It is another way of pointing to the universal which was referred to in the last chapter. It is necessary to be that which we are or, in the way I describe it, to create that which we are. We have to become it and this again echoes Bion who said we have to become *O*.

This metaphysical orientation was germane to those Russian thinkers, known as the slavophiles in the last half of the nineteenth century, especially Dostoievsky, Tolstoy, and Solovyov. (The psychoanalyst who shares this orientation is Bion who called this totality *O*.) There was a definite cleavage between the metaphysics of these thinkers and of their contemporaries, like Belinsky in Russia but also thinkers in Germany, France, England, and Austria. I mention Austria last because here was Freud rooted in this passionate dogmatism which spread like an epidemic through the medical schools of Europe. For these Russians there was a oneness in the diversity, and the *harmony* that Solovyov speaks of is rooted in that oneness, in that totality and that this knowledge is through intuition. The different parts within the personality have this coherence intrinsically, and the light that I referred to is the intuition that penetrates into it. In the absence of this light the different parts are united but only through external attachment and this leads to the poison that I spoke of, but we need to understand why this is.

I shall examine first the two modes of connection between one human being and another and then see how this symbolises the internal relations. There are two ways in which I can relate to this other human being beside me. Either I can focus my eyes upon her and let her draw my being to her so that she becomes my *ego*, as it were, or I close my eyes and let my being be drawn by a creative power within. I am careful here not to call this my own creative power. It possesses me and not me it. The manifestation of this creative power is in dreams and *reverie*. The reality which I share with all members of the human race is in me. I am part of the human race and this same Russian thinker, Solovyov, refers to this as the principle of *solidarity* and it is from this that sympathy is derived. This solidarity is another way of speaking of the universal experiens that all share (see Chapter Two, p. 5). So this individual who is here with me now has a sensual presence to me and me to her and this is the material upon which the creative power operates. My relation to her is now in this inner creative activity. Let us then call these two modes *relating* and *clinging*. In *clinging* mode there is at the same time fear of what is within. I *cling* to the other and yet it is not really an *I* but rather an assortment of bits being held together by a series of one sticking to the other. On the other hand if I am *relating* then the different parts are inwardly connected and so there is a true *I*. One can think of this in Winnicott's terms as there being a *potential space*.

Now these two different modes of connecting to the other are also the two ways in which the different parts link to one another within the personality. If the connections within are in *clinging* mode then that part which is undeveloped, is in infancy, will poison the rest of the personality. But why? It is because fear thrusts outside itself that which is feared. The feared reality is ejected and this sets up a system of ejection among all the parts. The sign that this is the situation is the presence of *shame*. *Shame* is a declaration pointing to this inner poisoned state of affairs.

There is the relation of one to another at the sensory level and then the relation at the level of solidarity or universal experiences. At the sensory level the one is isolated from the other. In the inanimate world there are realities that are physically oppositional; one stone is not another; the one stone is outside the other. But there are realities built into the fabric of the physical world which are spiritual. Two examples: volume and weight. Volume is intrinsic to the objects and yet it is spiritual. The word *spirit* is a negatively defined concept. It means a reality that is not material. Volume is a spiritual reality. The spiritual reality that is more relevant for us is the *in-relation* of objects. Relatedness is intrinsic and yet it is spiritual. It cannot be measured or discovered through being weighed. Things at the sensory level are outside each other physically but there is an *in-relation*. This quality of *in-relation* exists intrinsically at the subatomic level as has been emphasised by Charles Birch. He says that an atom or molecule acquires different properties according to the nature of the surrounding system. A carbon atom in a diamond (composed of other carbon atoms) is different from a carbon atom in an enzyme. He says specifically:

> There is no reason why we should not say than an electron is attracted to a proton. We mean that the electron takes into account internally the proton in its environment. The proposition is that all entities such as electrons, cells and humans have internal relations. They can all be called organisms. (1995, p. 79)

In the inner constitution the one and the other are in relation. There is the sensory level and the ontological level. One isolated from the other is the sensory mode; inner to inner is at the ontological level. The sensory level is a connection of outer to outer; each is isolated from the other but this is no longer so once the sensory level is contained in being and this is the level which governs the whole. This is elaborated further in Chapter Ten.

The relation at the level of Being, Solidarity, or Universality transcends the sensory reality of each and, at the same time, is the deepest reality of each. This reality is creative and initiatory because it relates from its own inwardness. It takes account of the other in its own inwardness and as Charles Birch says the subatomic particle takes another subatomic particle *inwardly* into account.

There is within each of these inner functions an initiatory principle. I like the analogy of a seed that needs to be watered because it implies that the initiatory action needs to stem from within the seed but that it requires an outer inspiration for the process to start. We need to look at the psychological equivalent of water and sunlight. The difference between inanimate matter and living things is that in the latter there is a principle initiating action, however small a percentage of motion is attributable to this. In human beings it is this small bit of initiatory action that makes it personal. This backs up what I have held: that the creative principle is the core of the personality. It seems weak, almost invisible, a nothing that is yet everything. The French thinker, Maurice Blondel, writing in 1893, expressed this succinctly thus:

> If therefore the synthesis is something more than the immense multitude of its conditions, there has to be in it something to contain and dominate this very immensity; a remainder that no doubt is as little as nothing and which the sciences take into account only to eliminate it; but it is this nothing which, from an interior viewpoint, is everything, since it is the invisible principle of synthesis, the soul of all positive knowledge and of every efficacious operation. (1984, p. 98)

Small, weak, invisible—nothing and yet everything. Something not available to science but is captured by the arts. The novelist who did, I believe, capture this was George Meredith. In the prelude to his novel *The Egoist* he designates the "Comic Spirit" as the unifier: "… the inward mirror, the embracing and condensing spirit, is required to give us those interminable milepost piles of matter (extending well-nigh to the very Pole) in essence, in chosen samples, digestibly" (1919, p. 2). What Meredith recognises here is the way in which unification occurs through a selection which nevertheless is a faithful representation of a wide range of experience. As the novel unfolds he shows how the protagonist, Sir Willoughby Patterne, attempts to unify through subsuming his fiancée within his own restricted world. Rather than having a faith in an essence which is there in the wide world Sir Willoughby attempts to impose a unification that is based upon a shutting out of a transcendent principle that is in the world. This unification through annihilation occurs similarly when someone imposes the view of Freud, Klein, Bion, or Kohut upon the myriad stimuli that make up all human communication. The point I am making, or trying to make, has been made very well by the painter, André Lhote. He is referring to the way in which Cézanne broke new ground by finding structure through *not* turning to a theory, a chosen principle of order that pre-exists in the mind of the subject:

> For centuries the cultured Frenchman has been taught that order ought to precede the organisation of forms and colours, but not that passion, when it is unleashed in the transports of consciousness, may seek to base itself on a new order, ceaselessly invented, which will be nothing but the fixation of rhythm, even of its explosion. The Latin mentality doesn't appreciate this organisation sought in the heart of cataclysm. It needs *a priori* constructions, nice clean cages to imprison the birds of its imagination. It doesn't easily discern these unstable architectures, always renewed, which inspiration builds by trial and error. (1998, p. 179)

André Lhote has a faith that in the passion there is an order to be found rather than imposing one that annihates the magic vision. What Meredith refers to as the "Comic Spirit" or the "Inward Mirror" transcends the limited world of the individual's own precious world-annihilating method of unification.

Freud (1919a) also recognised that there was a synthesising principle in the personality. He says:

> ... the neurotic patient presents us with a torn mind, divided by resistances. As we analyse it and remove the resistances, it grows together; the great unity which we call his ego fits into itself all the instinctual impulses which before had been split off and held apart from it. The psycho-synthesis is thus achieved during analytic treatment without our intervention, automatically and inevitably. (1919, p. 161)

He implies here that the principle of unification is within the personality and does not come about through an external imposition. We can take the analogy of the reproductive cell in the organism. The nucleus of one cell fuses with the nucleus of the other producing a separate being from the parent nuclei.

The creative principle is linked then to a principle of selection. Of the myriad stimuli bombarding the organism only a few are selected, as George Meredith emphasises. These may be selected according to the pleasure principle or the ascetic principle. The pleasure principle guides the personality towards elements that are sensually attractive; the ascetic principle blinds the personality to those sensual elements in favour of invisible forms but these are *in* the elements without destruction of them, without annihilation of them just as volume does not destroy the elements into which it is bonded. Through *askesis* the senses are blinded so that the *nothing* can be captured. As already observed, this was central to Picasso's understanding. His "metaphorical inner eye" is the same as Meredith's "Comic Spirit" or "Inward Mirror" and Blondel's "nothing". The first two are its artistic expression; the latter its quasi-philosophical expression but they refer to the same thing. Blondel refers to it objectively; Picasso and Meredith refer to it subjectively.

These invisible forms suffuse and embrace the sensual elements which become included in these forms. The blinding of the senses characteristic of the ascetic principle enables the invisible forms to govern the process rather than vice versa.

It is when these forms, which themselves are fashioned by the creative principle, have accomplished their work of suffusing the sensual elements that the potential person becomes actually present; the potential is actualised. The person *is* this creation. The person *is* this *in-relation* permeating the whole personality. What George Meredith manages to convey through his analysis of the character of Sir Willoughby Patterne is the way in which the annihilation of all the world except himself and Clara, his betrothed, also annihilates that *inward mirror* and therefore shuts out himself. This is how Sir Willoughby tries to persuade Clara of this position:

> The world was the principal topic of dissension between these lovers. His opinion of the world affected her like a creature threatened with a deprivation of air. He explained to his darling that lovers of necessity do loathe the world. They live in the world, they accept its benefits, and assist it as well as they can. In their hearts they must despise it, shut it out, that their love for one another may pour in a clear channel, and with all the force thy have. They cannot enjoy the

sense of security for their love unless they fence away the world. "It is, you will allow, gross; it is a beast. Formally we thank it for the good we get of it; only we two have an inner temple where the worship we conduct is actually, if you would but see it, an excommunication of the world. We abhor that beast to adore that divinity. This gives us our oneness, our isolation, our happiness. This is to love with the soul. Do you see, darling?"

She shook her head; she could not see it. She would admit none of the notorious errors of the world; its backbiting, selfishness, coarseness, intrusiveness, infectiousness ... (1919, p. 45).

The *inward mirror* is synonymous with consciousness so the shutting out of the world is also a shutting out what is most elemental to his own being. Clara wants to break off her engagement to Sir Willoughby; her father does not understand why; Sir Willoughby does not understand why; Sir Willoughby is rich and has everything a young woman could want except ... and this is what Clara finds it so difficult to explain. How can she explain that Sir Willoughby lacks an *inward mirror*? It seems, like Blondel says, a mere *nothing* and yet it is everything.

This *inward mirror* is a creation but not only from within the individual but from a person outside. Is it possible for one person to create the *inward mirror* in another? I believe it is and this is the subject of the next chapter.

CHAPTER FIVE

Person generates person

We have already seen how the person is the outcome of the creative principle embracing the "givens" within the personality. But this creative principle is not confined within the individuality of one personality. Just as one cell generates another through a gene in its nucleus so one person generates another.

It is difficult to grasp the act of creation. It is something that we infer but cannot perceive. When we suddenly understand something, it is a manifestation of an unseen creative act. When we "realise" something for the first time, that is also the fruit of an inner act of creation. Something within has become transformed. Why it is difficult to grasp is that something is created and yet not caused. If it is truly created then it cannot be caused. This is because there is no source outside the creative act. It is the source. This is what creation means—something comes from this that has no antecedent cause. We are trapped within a causal system which is true of the inanimate world but it is not true of life, let alone human life. There is a powerful missionary spirit, which entraps a wider, a deeper vision within a lens, restricted to and appropriate to one portion of reality but not to the whole of the human condition, yet this limited perspective and its mode of functioning has been applied to the whole of reality. The source of a creative act lies in a nothing—*nothing*; it is a source that is nowhere.

The moment I think that this source is something which I possess then I have betrayed its nature. A misconception has occurred. The relationship cannot be possessed by either of the objects between which the relationship occurs. The act of creation partakes of the kind of reality instantiated in a relationship. The relation between events is there but again has to be created. That gravity is a principle of relation between all events of the physical universe—it was there but created by Newton. It is a created relation. There is a relationship between events within the personality which are created by the Newton within. I speak of the source but it is probably not quite the right imagery. The proper language for it is perhaps the *relation-source*. This mysterious activity within the personality is a reality, a wonder, to which I am servant. I try to become its master but this is something that I cannot do; I am its servant. I believe this is the meaning of the myth of Adam and Eve in the garden of Eden. Adam believed that this source of knowledge could become his possession. He ate of the fruit of the tree of knowledge. The serpent it was who insinuated that those two could become possessors of this source of knowledge. If this is right it means that from very ancient times wise elders have known through a deep intuition that the source of creativity is not something which can be possessed by human beings. I cannot possess my own creativity; I am possessed by it. The relationship between components within my personality cannot be possessed by me; the relationship between myself and others cannot, by definition, be my possession.

The act of understanding occurs in one person when the communication comes from the created element in another person. When it comes from the uncreated it is not understood either in the individual himself or in the other. Yet there is something in the interpersonal communication which is able to transform the uncreated into the created. So what if the element is uncreated in the analyst and in the patient? It is here that faith enters the picture. Belief is that psychological transformer which changes possibility into reality. It is the hen sitting on an egg. The egg has the possibility of becoming a baby chicken. The broody hen sitting on the egg enables the egg to become a baby chicken. Belief is of this nature. It can be in error. A hen can sit and sit on an unfertilised egg and no chick will ever appear. The element has to be capable of being transformed. Belief in the personality functions to bring about the transformation. The element has to be there for it to be transformed. Belief as a function becomes dysfunctional when belief becomes invested with an omnipotence that annihilates the element. Creation, in the human condition, is creation from something and of something, not creation from nothing. Only God can create from nothing. The recognition of the limitation of our faculties is the foundation for the healthy workings of the functions of our personality.

A theological student had heard from a lecturer that the epistles of St. Paul were written earlier than the four gospels. This was something which he knew and sat in his mind as a fact that floated unconnected to any other facts. Then a monk told him that the first revelation of Christ was through St. Paul's letters and he encouraged the student to read just those letters and put out of his mind the gospel texts. A light went on in the student's mind. This desiccated piece of information had now become real and his grasp of this aspect of the Christian revelation was real. The reason why there was this sudden illumination in the theological student was because the monk had assimilated this as a piece of personal understanding. It was not just a piece of academic knowledge for him but rather something that was of emotional significance to him. This easy phrase "emotional significance" needs some unpacking. What does it really mean? Let me come at this another way.

Madness is when something finite takes possession of the mind. Wisdom is when the infinite takes possession of the mind. But this is not the right phraseology. The mind finds its true end, loves its true end. The mind finds who she is in that act of loving its true end. The mind enters into relation with who she is. She becomes who she is. Madness is a mocking caricature of wisdom: where the finite captures the mind rather than the infinite. Wisdom is when the infinite captures the mind; madness is when the finite imprisons the mind.

I shall give another example from my own experience when I was in analysis. I had started attending clinical seminars. I had taken on my first patient. I spoke to my analyst of something occurring between me and my patient and said apologetically: "But I did not make a transference interpretation … ."

He asked me: "What is the purpose of making a transference interpretation?"

I fumbled and said feebly, "Well it … it … institutes psychic change."

There was a silence and then he spoke: "It is to remove an obstacle that exists between the analyst and the patient."

This seemingly simple statement had an enormous impact upon me. If one defines an interpretation as a statement that has a deep effect upon one's emotional being then this was a very powerful interpretation. It was not an intellectual statement; it was a personal one and had been arrived at through pain and distress. An act of understanding had happened in him, my analyst. It was because it was a personal act of understanding for him that it had so great an impact upon me. The personal creative act in him had created an element in me that until that moment was uncreated. The uncreated became created. I had not until that moment understood why a transference interpretation was so important a feature of psychoanalysis. In this moment I realised that the transference was a means and not an end; that the goal of psychoanalysis was to bring the creative centre of two persons into relation with each other and that the aim of the transference interpretation was to dissolve the sensual delusion that prevents the opening of the centre of one person to that of another.

A patient was in his sitting room at home putting stamps into his stamp album when he suddenly realised that his analyst did not know him completely and never would. An illusion was at that moment banished. The question here is this: if the analyst had himself believed that it was possible for him to know his patient completely would that realisation have occurred in his patient? I think it is very likely that it would not have happened. This moment of illumination happened in him because the analyst knew that he could never know his patient or any human being; that his knowledge both of himself and his patients was extremely limited; that he could only have transient glimpses of the other's inner world. So there was a connecting thread between the person of the analyst and the person of the patient. Even that may not be quite correct. It is that the person of the analyst created this new person in the patient. Understanding is a manifestation of this creation.

A psychiatrist was treating a young man who believed that she knew all that he was thinking. In discussion with her supervisor the psychiatrist realised for the first time the patient's belief that she knew all his thoughts without him having to speak them. The psychiatrist understood this for the first time. The understanding passed from the supervisor to the psychiatrist. What had been created in the supervisor transmitted to the psychiatrist. There was a time when the supervisor had not understood this. It was an arduous creative work that brought about the realisation in the supervisor. This passed later to the psychiatrist. Later still it passed to the young man whom the psychiatrist was treating.

This implies that one person can create in the other. This is possible because there is a call from the uncreated for creation. The uncreated is the world of which the other is a part; the place of the creative power is of no consequence to the uncreated. The individual is subservient to this power. It was this that Adam and Eve tried to subvert. The person is not a fixed entity whose boundaries are coterminous with the individual's physical frame. The power of creation lies in the relationship. The relationship which binds the two individuals is the power, the creative power, of which the individuals are servants. This current can occur when two people are at a physical distance from one another geographically or at a distance from one another in historical time, as in the example given from Tolstoy's *Anna Karenina* in Chapter Two.

This view is supported by quantum mechanics which shows that the presence of the observer affects the observed datum. It is also something which has been given potent expression in south Indian mythology.

One person can create in the other outside physical space or time. An analyst says to a patient:

> When you were telling me that your brother is unable to look after himself although he is thirty-five years old I think you were wanting to indicate that there was some early learning that has not happened either for your brother or for you.

At the time of saying it the patient did not grasp it but later she heard her aunt saying,

> Your mother was always too busy to teach you and your brother how to dress, how to catch the bus to school. The two of you were always at a loss.

When her aunt told her that, she suddenly understood the meaning of her analyst's statement. This detail supplied by her aunt made incarnate the analyst's abstraction—*some early learning*—so that it created the realisation. The creative comes from a relation—here it is the relation between a speculative abstraction concerning early education and a chronicle from childhood. She was connected to her analyst at that moment although she was at home twenty miles away from her analyst's consulting room and it was three days after her analyst had said it but, nevertheless, she was connected to her analyst at that instant—through the *nothing* (see Blondel in Chapter Three), through the *metaphorical inner eye* (see Picasso in the Introduction).

The moment of realisation is the manifestation of the connection between herself and the person of her analyst. This can occur years later when the analyst is dead. Physical death does not obliterate the person. A realisation from an intervention of my analyst came to me thirty-five years after the event. There was at that moment a living communication between him and me although he had been dead for twenty-five years.

We are so used to the phenomenon of projective identification which is the discharge of uncreated bits or *beta elements*, to use Bion's term, either into another individual, into an organisation, or into an ideology, that the idea that something can be created in another is foreign to our thinking, at least within psychoanalysis. We are also so tied to a causality based on the notion that one thing is the result of another that we cannot conceptualise that something can come entirely from me and yet be a creation issuing from another. The mind cannot grasp it so rather than acknowledge the limitations of our mind we say that it cannot be so. There is a difference between a logical contradiction and a seeming antinomy. I want to illustrate this by narrating a mythological story that comes from south India.

Précis of the Simantini story

Two Brahmin boys, Sumedha and Samavan, wanted enough money to be able to marry. They knew that Queen Simantini gave money to bridal pairs about to be married so Samavan dressed as a woman and, together with Sumedha, went, along with a group of other couples, to Queen Simantini's palace. The queen immediately recognised that Samavan was a boy. She gave all the couples clothes, scents, and jewels, praised them as Shiva and Uma and then gave them leave to depart.

On their way home Samavan turned into a woman. She turned to Sumedha and said, "Husband, I am burning with desire, please make love to me. If you refuse to make love to me I shall die." Sumedha examined her carefully and saw that she was a woman and a beautiful one at that. He was astonished and said, "Look, I came here with my friend, Samavan, but I don't see him any longer. Who are you?" She replied,

"I was your friend, Samavan, but I am now a woman and my name is Sarasvati."

At first Sumedha thought he was being tricked but Sarasvati undressed and revealed her whole body to him and then he was convinced. He then realised that this transformation had happened through the power of the imagination which Queen Simantini had exercised in her heart upon him on Monday, Shiva's Day.

The force inside imagination is called *bhavana* in Sanskrit. This way of thinking about the imagination is reminiscent of Montaigne (1991) who wrote about the power of the imagination and gives the example of a woman who turned into a man.

We need to reflect on this from different perspectives. The imagination is *transitive* and *interpersonal*. It is rooted in a belief which is not individualistic. Shiva is the god of the absolute. It is this participation of all being in the absolute, the source of all power, which endows the imagination with its huge strength. This transitive quality of the imagination is what is operating in Queen Simantini but the story indicates that its power comes from Shiva and his wife Uma. Queen Simantini becomes the human agent of Shiva. The cult of Shiva embodies the belief in an absolute which is the source of all creative power.

Creations of the imagination are facts. They are the only certain facts. The only facts which can be known. I only truly know that which I have created. If I sit down and paint a scene in front of me it is subjective in that anyone else painting the same scene will construct it differently. One can see an example of this in the paintings done by Cézanne and Camille Pissaro of the same scene. They sat beside each other and painted what they saw in front of them but Cézanne's painting is strikingly different from Pissaro's, yet one can instantly see that they were looking at the same house and trees that confronted each of them. All the stimuli that bombard the human subject are processed through a lens which fashions a construction out of the mass of stimuli.

Bhavana, the imagination, is the core of the self (*atma-guna*). It is through the power of *bhavana* that I construct the continuity of my own self. Memory (*smrti*) is the fruit of *bhavana* and so is recognition (*pratyabhijna*). When I recognise something in someone I am doing more than just a passive seeing; the act of seeing has a reconstructive force. It is the reason why a patient is often afraid of allowing something in himself to be seen. Attention (*ådara*) is also a bringing of something into being. In *bhavana* there is a formative power. It looks as though Queen

Simantini has transformed Samavan without any co-operation of his own volition and yet one has to ask why did Samavan dress up as a girl and not Sumedha? There was some sympathy within him for the feminine. There was a knowledge of the feminine that came from the psychic woman inside him, from the *anima*, to use Jung's word for it. Queen Simantini, by paying attention (*ādara*) to this hidden element inside Samavan, brings it into being. One might think that Samavan, through dressing up as a woman, invites Queen Simantini to give her attention to that hidden seed within him. Once she has become Sarasvati her desire for Sumedha to make love to her is so strong that this endorses the view that there was all along an active wish to become a woman. First he dresses as a woman and then, once become a woman, she is on fire with desire to be made love to. So the transformation has come about through an interactive process. Does it mean that there was all along a female "core self" in Samavan/Sarasvati which Queen Simantini's recognition (*pratyabhijna*) brings to birth? If this is so then the imagination functions by bringing a seed to life. Imagination then is in close alliance with belief, which is like a broody hen which brings the chick out of the egg. We are so used to the phenomenon where a bird sits on the egg and brings a baby chick out of the fertilised ovum that we do not marvel at this amazing power to bring new life from what seems to be a formless yoke at the centre of the egg. There is a knowledge in the south Indian culture that *bhavana* works. The Western use of the word "magic" is a cultural contempt for something which it does not understand and is not able to use properly.

These modes of being, *ādara* and *pratyabhijna*, attention and recognition, are not passive states but rather have active power, a *formative* power, as Newman (1927) says and, as David Shulman says (2005), they are *transitive*. Putting together these two we say that they have a power that is *transitive* and *formative*; that it is a power that forms, shapes, and binds scattered things into one; that the activity of attention has a fertilising strength inside it that passes from one mind to another. *Pratyabhijna* makes something which has been on the outer perimeter of the personality into the centre and fashions it into a principle that organises and unites the personality around it. It moves from being small and trifling in the inner hierarchy into a principle of supreme significance, like a member of Parliament who was on the back benches now being made prime minister.

In the story there is struggle and doubt. Sumedha does not believe that Samavan has become Sarasvati. He cannot believe in this transitive and formative power. It seems that attention is a surface touching and not a transforming gaze that pierces into the essence of the other.

I am in an art gallery and I walk along with a transient glance at each painting. Then I stop and do not glance but look and see this painting in front of me. I look at the dead body of a man being handled into the arms of two angels. One of the angels is looking forlorn and betrayed, let down by the dead man; the other is concerned with how the bystanders are thinking of him. The expression on the man's dead face is of accomplished surrender. The woman on the right, at the foot of the cross with outstretched arms, is having an hysterical fit whereas the woman on the left side knows what has happened and is crying softly. Then my eyes withdraw and reassemble the whole scene. I have now moulded these different parts into an inner experience of sadness, tragedy, and beauty. This looking at the painting is as different from the previous glancing as seeing the surface of the sea and going scuba diving with goggles and looking at all the coral, fish, crabs, and seaweed. There is a formative seeing; a seeing that creates what is there. And this is transitive—it can pass and does pass from one to another. There is a struggle to come to this belief. It is painful to give up the attachment to a familiar set of assumptions. Sumedha holds onto it. To see Sarasvati rather than Saravan he has to undergo a change in himself just as profound as has occurred to Saravan/Sarasvati. Saravan is a young man; he sees him in a particular way, in a fixed way; the inner pattern is moulded in concrete. To see what has happened requires a breakdown of the way the building inside has been constructed. It has to be pulled down and put together again. He cannot believe that this inner has changed, that Queen Simantini has exercised this power of *pratyabhijna* upon the inner being of Saravan. He can only believe it by allowing the creative power now to change him.

The German mystic, Meister Eckhart, says that detachment is greater than love.

> ... why I praise detachment more than humility is that perfect humility bows down beneath all creatures, and this bending down man goes out of himself and into the creatures. But detachment remains within itself. Now no going out can ever be so noble as the indwelling is in itself. (1963, p. 157)

He means, I believe, detachment from an immovable, unchangeable imprint of the inner contours of the other. It is necessary to detach from the inner building as it is constructed and allow it to be reconstituted. It is detachment from what is there and an imaginative construction of a different building within. For this to happen the old one has to be knocked down first. The view that there is a fixed static state outside me that conditions the me—this has to be overthrown. It is the source of madness. It is what is most deeply me that has to be created. The stimulus-response view of the behavioural psychologist has to be overthrown. This is the belief that the human organism is entirely shaped by the stimuli that bombard it. The view that the human person is subject to the infinite rather than the finite allows for plasticity whereas the latter attachment solidifies what needs to be flexible. This needs further elaboration.

There are two dimensions to every single thing, whether it be a star like Sirius, a mineral like copper, a flower like a dandelion, an animal like a leopard, a human child, an old woman, a dream, an historical event like the Second World War, or a religious ritual like the celebration of the Eucharist in the Catholic Church. One is the surface which can be described or narrated, the other is its existence which transcends and, at the same time, is *in* the thing or event. The latter is undefined except by its existence. There is no restricting factor. A flower is not an animal but the only thing which existence is not is non-existence. If I sink my surface, sensation-based individuality into my existence I am in brotherhood with the stars, the minerals, the plants, the animals, human beings, and all historical events. If I become the infinite then I am open to all reality of which I am a part. I am plastic; I am flexible. If I sink myself into my individually shaped piece of human reality then I am inflexible and rigid. The human person is in the existence which I "sink into" through an act of creative insight. To the extent to which I merge this essence into my own individual shape thus am I fashioned by the implosion of finite elements that bombard me.

This sinking of the essence into my own individual shape fashions, then, my mode of attachment. This *sinking of the essence* becomes the template for my mode of relating to … other people, to religious denominations, to political organisations, to psychological schools, to socialism, to neuroscience, to psychoanalysis. I merge my personal being into the social body and lose my own judgment upon it. I become its slave rather than exercise my own discernment towards it. Rather than relate from my centre to the governing principles of the organisation I submerge under the chaos of its laws and dictates.

There is a connection between *bhavana* and language. The naming of something is not just representing what is there but creating what is there. The naming is also a shaping of what is there. The word, the naming, is also a selecting of a limited range of elements in either the external or internal world and framing them. It is a leaving aside of some things and taking others and framing them with language. Language then is *bhavana's* instrument. One can think of the whole world as being in a process of emergence and *bhavana* with language as her instrument bringing the fresh new world to birth. Another way of thinking about it is to consider music. When listening to music there is attention (*ādara*) to pre-semantic vibrations. The naming also then fixes a sequence into a permanent recordable shape. So *bhavana* together with language fashions object in the human world.

Bhavana in order to work has first to melt down what is there, break it down into its elements before it can reconstruct it. There is also the notion that the imagination aims at something and this something is Shiva with his wife Uma. *Bhavana* is a becoming of Shiva. *Bhavana* or imagination is the instrument through which Shiva acts. Shiva is the ultimate or the depth of which *bhavana* is the effective instrument. Shiva can create from nothing; *bhavana* creates from the broken up elements. There is this sense then that *bhavana* is working towards a goal, a *telos*, and this is why the analogy of the seed, which *ripens* into a goal but one which, though definite, is indeterminate, is apposite.

I become what I am in the mind of Truth. I become this through a creative act. I am then a servant to this new being that I have become. But I am a servant, not a slave.

CHAPTER SIX

Meaning as the subjective experience of unity

In Chapter One I mentioned that the creative principle, apart from transforming "givens", also generates a unity; that those disparate parts are now parts of one whole. This is possible, as stated in Chapter One, because the creative principle is, in its essence, both transcendent and immanent. Its structure is able to "*in-form*" a series of facts because, being mental, it can penetrate the physical form of existence. This is why I named it the "*all-inclusive principle*"—in that it is a oneness that is in diversity of inner and outer stimuli. Like volume, weight, or density it permeates all the elements, is *in* all the elements, without either adding or detracting from them.

Meaning is the subjective experience of this unity. Bion (1962) says that a particular fact illuminates an array of what had before been disjointed facts. He called this unifying principle the "selected fact". It is a mistake, however, to think of this as a fact such as a sensation which can never be unifying in the way he suggests. Psychological factors that have the same permeable quality as volume, weight, or density are grief, disappointment, longing, hope, despair, shame, goodness, or truth. It is a mental principle which infuses the sensual imagery. Grief, disappointment, hope, goodness, creativity, or truth are realities not ideas. So the "*all-inclusive principle*" is as real as a stone or a crocodile

63

but without physical characteristics. It is psychic reality rather than material reality. Freud (1940b) refers to psychical reality though does not emphasise it.

This understanding of meaning is deeper than that proposed by analytic philosophy which interprets it according to the linguistic structure of the sentence. This defines meaning according to surface description. There is a refusal in this philosophy to penetrate below the surface. There is a hatred in it of metaphysical intuition. I have already (see Chapter One) quoted Polanyi's pellucid assertion of this.

Other examples of mental principles are trust and love, with pain as included in love. Because love opens the mind to a wider perspective it includes painful things which had been excluded on the narrower canvas. This frame which shuts out both faculties within the mind and also unifying principles outside the mind is the consequence of hatred. Love opens the personality to the whole of existence; hatred shuts out this totality. It is a hatred of this totality which makes me so small. I am a fragment of existence. Love shows me my own smallness within the totality of the universe but the marvel of the whole infuses this small fragment which I call *I*. Hatred which shuts out the totality has the effect of making the fragment into the whole. It is the fashioner then of a delusion. The sign that hatred is at work in the personality is that certain inner faculties and outer principles are viciously shut out. I shall give an example of this.

A middle-aged woman came for psychoanalysis because … well, various reasons were given. She felt alienated from her mother and father and also her brother. She said that she thought there was something wrong about it. When treatment started she complained bitterly about both her mother and father. Her mother had put her in a home when she was aged three. Her brother was not born at that point. She was in the home for four months. Her father was in the diplomatic service and he was going on a very important mission to India and her mother was so keen to accompany him that she put her baby, Louisa, into foster care in a residential home for orphans. She referred again and again to the cruelty of a nurse who was there. This nurse used to stand over her and force her to eat her food very quickly.

She would suddenly speak to me with one hurried sentence: "I think Teresa, my secretary, does not like me," and then she would stop. She would drop the sentence into the room as if it had floated in like a spaceship from the sky. There was five minutes of silence before she spoke and then ten minutes again after speaking. The atmosphere was tense. I felt impelled to speak. I wanted to ask: "What do you think it is that she does not like about you?" The pressure for me to say this was immense. If I had surrendered to this invisible force it would have been against my will, against my desire. I did not but what if I had done? How would the interaction between us have been different? It would have been an exchange where what came forth from me would not have been from my own inner desire but rather from something pressed out of me against my own inner being. What about on her side? I believe that this silent but unseen power also did not come from her own inner desire but rather that she too was under a force. So, had I given in to this nameless force, there would have been in the consulting room an interaction between two pre-programmed computers. I believe that when she repeatedly spoke of those four months when she was in a residential home for orphans, she did so because there shone out from that soul-destroying event an atomic radiation of shattering power that overcame her inner autonomy, her own inner self, that inner being that she would refer to as "me"; the "me" that lay in ruins and scattered.

After blundering many times and offering questions of this sort I stayed quiet and slowly I gathered that she was unable to generate any thoughts of her own, any reflections upon herself. So, for instance, she said, "There's a woman called Emily and she organises everyone at the bridge club," and then—silence. A pause of five minutes and then: "My mother used to make me do things that I did not want to do." I said, "You speak of two women who like bossing people around." She said, "Oh, so you think I am like that." I had become slave to this hidden pressure. It becomes clear slowly that she cannot reflect upon her managerial ways of behaving. She is only able to have it as an authoritative voice that tells her she has a bossy way of behaving and commanding her not to. The capacity to generate a realisation is almost absent or, at the very least, poorly developed. There is a melancholy that governs her mood and behaviour and as we probe more deeply into her emotional life we find that the reason for it is the absence of an inner authority. She is unable to create from within. She is suffering from the absence of this within her. The historian Arthur Bryant has expressed it thus:

> Man is by nature, a producer or creator as well as a consumer, and unless the instinct to create and produce implanted in him by nature is satisfied, he will to a greater or lesser degree, be an

unsatisfactory and discontented being … If man is not given the opportunity to create, he will, in his unconscious frustration, destroy. (1969, pp. 268–269)

So the mental principle here is the loss of the creative principle through that disaster that occurred to her when she was aged three. The loss of inner authority is the mental principle that underlies the variety in the descriptive account she gives of her difficulties. Inner authority is a kind of birthright and when we have been robbed of it through early catastrophes there remains a mental illness as a sign of this elemental loss. So the *all-inclusive principle* is the loss of inner authority. Creativity, as one of the basic mental principles, is synonymous with inner authority.

This explained her hatred of her mother, father, and brother. The nature of this hatred needs to be examined. It is not that the mother is seen and hated but that her individual existence is clearly within perception and that her subjective existence is wiped out. The woman in question knew that her mother existed in the way that she knew the city of London existed, what a tomato looks like, that there was once a man called Napoleon, that we are living in the twenty-first century. She knew her mother existed as a fact. Her knowledge was external. She could have given an outer description of her mother. Her knowledge was of the outer surface of things. Her knowledge was not of the kind that penetrates into the inner life of the other. Her hatred had wiped this out. So her mother was like a walking robot.

I was once supervising a therapist who was treating a woman called Alice who lived with Jonas, her partner. She had lived with Jonas for four years. She was frustrated with him. He was depressed and it irritated her, not that she realised that he was depressed. When she got home he would be lounging in front of the television. She reproached him for not getting supper ready. He forgot to service the car so it came to a stop because the oil had not been changed. He had not got promotion in his job so his salary was small. Alice shouted at him, what sort of man he was, he was hampering her life, her career, and her chances of having a baby. How could she have a baby with a man who lounged around and did nothing to provide for her? He was an obstacle in her life and then suddenly one day she announced to her therapist: "I have suddenly realised that Jonas has feelings." Until that moment he had been a robot. Her hatred had, until that moment, shut out intuitive knowledge. Jonas, until that moment, was only known to the extent that he either frustrated or satisfied her. That he had an inner life was unknown to her. She had not realised that he felt disappointment, was hurt when she shouted at him. Until that moment he was not a subject in her consciousness.

It is worth reflecting on the fact that until that sudden illumination Jonas was only known to Alice to the extent to which he either frustrated or satisfied her. Her inner philosophy that guided her was of someone who sought pleasure and avoided pain. This was her goal in life. Seeking pleasure and avoiding pain was what motivated her. This motivational system is not concerned with how the pleasure is achieved or how the pain is avoided. If the pleasure is achieved at the cost of someone else's well-being this is of no consequence. If the pain is avoided by ignoring the distress of another then so be it. Yet this is the motivational system which we inherit from Freud. It was not Freud who invented it. He himself inherited it from psycho-physical philosophy which he imbibed from his mentor, Ernst Brücke who was a founding member of the *Physicalische Gesellschaft*. Underlying this philosophy was the view that humans are impelled by outer stimuli in the same way in which inanimate matter is. So the ego in Freud's schema is a passive slave to the perceptual stimuli and instinctive impulses from within but, I am putting forth the idea that imagination, *bhavana*, is the core of the self. It is not that imagination just transforms the human world in fancy or in an idea but that it truly constructs our world.

The seeking of pleasure and avoidance of pain are the subjective registration of differential stimuli hitting the organism through the medium of the senses. The stimulus that produces pleasure is the one that determines the direction in which the organism goes; the stimulus that provokes pain steers the organism away from its epicentre. It is at the deepest level a passive state. The passive state is a self-enclosed one. So this is a philosophy born of someone in the same emotional state that Alice was in before her moment of illumination. It is only through activity that the intuition into the subjectivity of the other is achieved. In the passive state there is no concern with the object which causes the pain; it could be a wasp stinging me or someone pricking me with a needle. Under this system it is of no concern. It was John Henry Newman who emphasised the formative quality of the mind, which I have referred to in the last chapter.

If I am sensitive to the distress of another it is because I go out of myself but it requires what Newman refers to as an enlargement of mind. This means that my mind undergoes a re-formation. The move from passive to active requires an inner reconstruction of the mental contents.

I want now to compare what I am saying here with the two states described by Melanie Klein as the *paranoid-schizoid position* and the *depressive position*. The former position was first named the *paranoid position* by Klein but, under the influence of Fairbairn, she renamed it the *paranoid-schizoid* position. *Schizoid* means a withdrawn, self-enclosed state. As Alice was outside the arena of Jonas's subjectivity she was therefore in a *schizoid* position but she is also tormented by Jonas's behaviour which was called *paranoid* by Klein. So she was both withdrawn into herself and persecuted by Jonas's passive state. This is the state of mind which generated the determinist philosophy which sees human beings as driven by inner instincts and outer stimuli with no originating source from within the living person. It is a passive state of mind. The mind as a formative power, such as Newman describes, is closer to Melanie Klein's *depressive position*. The emphasis here is upon the guilt that someone feels when there is a realisation that the object (Jonas in the example I am following) is suddenly seen to be not just a breast that satisfies or frustrates but that attached to that breast is a person who can and has been hurt and injured (by Alice). But Newman adds something to what Melanie Klein has given us. He says that the mind is an active formative power but this is linked to an enlargement of mind. This enlargement of mind through contact with a transcendent, though at the same time immanent principle is one that embraces not just the other as a person but also the subject as a person, because until that propitious moment it was not only that Alice saw Jonas just as an object that satisfied or frustrated her, but she also herself became more than an object determined by such states, as a formative constructor of events, and that these two were embraced in the unity of being.

This is the place in someone out of which unity is constructed. What I mean is that this consciousness of the subjectivity of the other is the unifying principle. Kant said that the *noumenon* was unknowable but Schopenhauer believed, and I think correctly, that the *noumenon* is that inner personal act; that the subjective is the noumenon. Alice had lost that through a calamity in her own life. She had been adopted. She had lost through that unhappy event her capacity to intuit the inner life of another. It is that when someone has been drowned under the impact of a cataclysm then she is subject to the impact of the outer until someone, friend or therapist, has arrived at sympathetic understanding of that original disaster. This understanding is not just a sympathetic understanding of what happened many years before but recognising that her cruelty towards Jonas (and towards her analyst) was the disaster active in the present. Only then can the individual be free of the victim state. The therapist had been in sympathetic union with Alice in those early disasters that she had suffered. It was when Alice truly knew that her analyst had understood her that Jonas, who had until then just been an object, became for her a person with feelings. It was through her analyst's understanding, which is a synonym for a shared-ness, that the therapist penetrated into her own suffering state so Alice experienced herself as a person and concurrently saw Jonas as a person. When she saw Jonas as a person it was a sign that her own personhood had come to birth within her. She sees Jonas through the lens of her own being. She knows herself as a person *through inference* when she sees Jonas as a person. In other words she does not *feel* herself as a person but *knows* it through inference. This is what Schopenhauer meant—it is unknown in that it is not accessible through feelings but by inference. This is a better way of saying it than to say it is a knowledge which is unconscious rather than conscious. The implication of this is that the other and the self are in a shared reality. It is what I have referred to elsewhere as *participated being* (Symington, 2004, pp. 77–84). When there is understanding of something the very understanding changes the nature of the something. A loss and a loss understood are two different things. We have already observed that understanding is the manifestation of an inner creative act. So loss which is an element in the personality, either an event or the consequence of an event, is created. The creative principle has been established. The way I am expressing myself here implies that there is always present in the personality a creative principle so that even a loss can be transformed. The way I have been stating this is to suggest that the inner authority was lost through the disaster this woman went through when her mother put her in an institution at the age of three. But now it begins to look as though this cannot be true because she is able to understand the loss, the absence, the barely formed element. But we come here to the purpose of psychoanalysis, the purpose of psychotherapy. I have stressed the transitive nature of mental states, of mental capacities. If this creative principle is present, is active in the analyst, then it can stimulate the same creative principle spontaneously into being. This was the subject of the last chapter.

When this capacity for generating it is absent it becomes replaced with a substitute: an outer command, an outer theory, an outer figure who is falsely made into the maker of unity. So she cannot reflect upon her emotional behaviour towards others. Patients who come for analysis have been functioning with substitute principles but there is an inchoate knowledge that this is not satisfactory. They are coming to look for the psychoanalyst together with her to create this principle within. Just as Queen Simantini created the desire to be feminine in Samavan into a fully-fledged reality, so the analyst creates the desire in the patient into an established reality at the same time as knowing, through inference, that he is establishing it in himself. A word about desire. The presence of desire I think indicates that there is a seed already present—a seed that needs watering. I suspect that this desire requires purifying. Desire, as we all know, can be very base but I think the more the "level of desire" is raised the more it has the capacity to "fertilise" and bring into life the seed. The purer the desire the more potent it is in bringing to bear that which is desired.

Then there are principles uniting both the internal and external world. Such a principle again is desire whose object is the achievement of unity. Emotional growth means progress from disjointed diversity to harmony and oneness. This is present even when the external representation seems to be furthest from it. It is this creative principle that creates the unity and it is an adjoining principle that establishes that unity so that it does not flash like lightning across the night sky of the mind but becomes a permanent possession. Again, Newman (1927) says:

> … such knowledge is not a mere extrinsic or accidental advantage, which is ours today and another's tomorrow, which may be got up from a book, and easily forgotten again, which we can command or communicate at our pleasure, which we can borrow for the occasion, carry about in our hand, and take to the market; it is an acquired illumination, it is a habit, a personal possession, and an inward endowment. (p. 113)

Freud implied that the relationship between the untransformed "givens" and the coherent part of the personality is what produces the conflict that generates neurosis. He also infers that there are "givens" in the unconscious which do not arise through repression; in other words not through any act of ours. This means that there are elements in the personality requiring our creation. They are there, not because they have been repressed but because we have not yet created them. In fact, he shifted his focus so that the conflict in the personality was no longer between consciousness and the unconscious but rather between a coherent part of the personality and incoherent parts: "When we find ourselves thus confronted by the necessity of postulating a third Ucs., which is not repressed, we must admit that the characteristic of being unconscious begins to lose significance for us" (Freud, 1923b, p. 18).

The incoherent parts are unconscious but that is a consequence of their incoherence. It is therefore the incoherence that is of primary importance. The making of the unconscious/conscious primary has been the cause of misunderstanding within psychoanalytic discourse. It is the error which the mediaeval scholar and mystic, Meister Eckhart, warned of when he said: "To regard as primary what is secondary is the 'root of all fallacy'" (Kelley, 1977, p. 42).

Now Freud (1923b) makes it clear what is primary in the following passage:

> From the point of view of analytic practice, the consequence of this discovery [that there are elements in the Ucs that have not arisen through repression] is that we land in endless obscurities and difficulties if we keep to our habitual forms of expression and try, for instance, to derive neuroses from a conflict between the conscious and unconscious. We shall have to substitute for this antithesis another, taken from our insight into the structural conditions of the mind—the antithesis between the coherent ego and the repressed which is split off from it … we must admit the characteristic of being unconscious begins to lose significance for us. (p. 18)

Subsequent to this last remark he says that nevertheless we must beware of ignoring the difference between something that is conscious as opposed to unconscious because he says it is, "… in the last resort our one beacon-light in the darkness of depth-psychology".

A beacon-light points to something other than itself. It is this other something that became for Freud at this point in his thinking the core of the matter whereas conscious or unconscious were manifestations, symptoms if you like, of a more central issue. It is interesting to watch Freud's thought process here. Here the great champion of the unconscious says: "We must admit the characteristic of being unconscious begins to lose significance for us" (1923b, pp. 17–18). But then he does not quite dare to push ahead to what this amazing statement implies but falls back on what is familiar for him. He is of course quite right that the difference between something of which we are aware and something of which we are unaware is huge, as I emphasised in the last chapter. But what he points to here is that consciousness and what is unconscious is the phenomenon of which the noumenon is coherence as opposed to that which is incoherent. He maintains here that what is separate from the ego is repressed or split off. This implies that it has been shut off from the ego. Yet he defines repression in the paper with that title (*The Ego and the Id*) as the removal of attention from an element in the personality. There is something there from which attention is absent. It is likely that he does not quite say that there are elements in the personality which are separate from the coherent ego without having been split off, because this is what Jung held and it was one of the theoretical issues on which the two men parted. That Freud had come round to Jung on this important matter was something which was very difficult for the master to acknowledge.

So what Freud is asserting here is that the conflict is between that which is coherent from that which is incoherent. The coherence comes from an inner principle of creativity, inner authority, generosity, love, forgiveness, and gratitude. It is this inner principle that fashions coherence. Meaning arises from this coherence; that the elements are bound together through this inner principle. That which is incoherent is meaningless. When a patient says something that makes sense for him it has become meaningful; it unites something in herself. Sheer destruction or unintegration is meaningless. Destructiveness always requires an inner principle of coherence to make it meaningful.

Freud himself never formulates the proposition that there is a powerful internal desire to unify the disparate elements in the personality. It is implied in what has been quoted above but he does not push through to the logic behind it. This, I think, is because he steers away from any metaphysical principle. He was opposed to religion or to what he referred to as any *Weltanschaungen*. To what principle does the desire for unity belong?

This desire for unity can be achieved in two different ways: through the *all-inclusive principle* or through the adoption of an outer membrane which holds the contents together without any informing principle.

In this latter mode there is no inner relation between the elements but rather what joins the disparate elements together is like a tarpaulin used to cover a series of objects: potatoes, an engine, and some books. The psychic tarpaulin might be, for instance, Kleinian theory, Winnicottian theory, or self-psychology. So, in the former, phantasy, the paranoid-schizoid position, and the death instinct are under the Klein tarpaulin; in the latter transitional objects, the good-enough mother, the true and false self, and psychosis as an environmental deficiency disease are under the Winnicott tarpaulin, and under self-psychology: attunement, mirroring, and self-objects. What unites them in each case is not an internal principle but rather that they were formulated by a particular individual. That individual may have had an internal principle that united them all for him or her but this is not so for the disciples. For this to be so an inner act of understanding grasping the *all-inclusive principle* would be necessary, but once this has been personally achieved then the person who has generated this is already his or her own person and no longer in servitude to the maestro. So, desire for unity can be satisfied in either of these two ways, but it is only the method which is arrived at through an inner personal grasp of a mental principle that illuminates all the variety without any annihilation. Paul Tillich has expressed this clearly:

> ... truths, once deep and powerful, discovered by the greatest geniuses through profound suffering and incredible labour, become shallow and superficial when used in daily discussion. How can and how does this tragedy occur? It can and does unavoidably occur, because there can be no depth without the way to the depth. The truth without the way to truth is dead; if it is still used, it contributes only to the surface of things. Look at the student who knows the content of the hundred most important books of world history, and yet whose spiritual life remains as shallow as it ever was, or perhaps becomes even more superficial. And then look at an uneducated worker who performs a mechanical task day by day, but who suddenly asks himself: "What does it mean, that I do this work? What does it mean for my life? What is the meaning of my life?" Because he asks these questions, that man is on the way into depth, whereas the other man, the student of history, dwells on the surface among petrified bodies, brought out of the depth by some spiritual earthquake of the past. The simple worker may grasp

truth, even though he cannot answer his questions; the learned scholar may possess no truth, even though he knows all the truths of the past. (1964b, pp. 61–62)

The crucial words here are *there can be no depth without the way to the depth*. It is the difference between an act of understanding that grasps the inner uniting principle and the surface ingestion of a series of dicta. This same point has been made by Michael Polanyi:

> … the traveller, equipped with a detailed map of a region across which he plans his itinerary, enjoys a striking intellectual superiority over the explorer who first enters a new region—yet the explorer's fumbling progress is a much fairer achievement than the well-briefed traveller's journey. Even if we admitted that an exact knowledge of the universe is our supreme mental possession it would still follow that man's most distinguished act of thought consists in *producing* such knowledge … (1959, p. 18).

There is innate knowledge of my scattered state within; shame is the feeling, most fundamental of all feelings, that registers the inner uncoordinated bits and pieces within the personality. Therefore there is a desire for wholeness, for unity of my being. I can solve it then either by generating an *all-inclusive principle* or thrusting my disparate bits into a prefabricated tarpaulin. I shall call the first mode of achieving my desire *personal desire* and the second *individualistic impulse*.

There are two currents in our lives. One is our animal heritage whose final goal is survival. But survival of what? Is it my survival? My own individual survival is servant to a purpose which is beyond my own individuality. It refers to the continuance of the species of which the individual is a component part. Like a relay race the individual's job is to pass the baton on … to another who will pass it on to another and so on. The goal is not even the continuity of the species. As we know from Darwin there is development within species. A species as it exists today is not the same as it was five million years ago. So it would seem that the goal is not just continuity but rather that it is heading somewhere towards something whose outline is not clear at the moment. Darwin teaches that each species is evolving. The word *hominisation* refers to that transformation, over a period of two million years, whereby apes became men. So this is one current: the evolving passageway of life and each individual's task is to pass that on. The individual does this through procreation and adaptation to the environment. But then there is another current where we are called to be a genius. The fact that only very few members of the human race receive the accolade of genius does not mean that it is not a human goal for everyone. We need now to examine carefully what is meant by genius.

I will quote first from Solovyov:

> Man as a moral being does not want to obey this natural law of *replacement* of generations, the law of *eternal death*. He does not want to be that which replaces and is replaced. He is conscious—dimly at first—both of the desire and the power to *include* in himself all the fullness of the *infinite life*. (1918, p. 138)

We can refer to a scientific genius, a literary, artistic, or musical genius, and a religious genius. Sometimes it is referred to as the divine spark within. What quite is meant by it? In any of these fields the sense of being a genius is to be a creator. Each genius, in any of these fields, is a creator, but of what? When Isaac Newton generated the theory of gravity he had, at that point, created within himself a principle uniting phenomena as different as an apple falling from a tree, the planets circling the sun, and the force which holds all of us to the ground. So genius also in the artistic or religious domain has this same unifying principle.

I have quoted Tillich but I want to adopt his language for a moment to give a different perspective on it. He says that the world is a mass of fragments of which I am one such fragment. I can either see the world through the lens of one fragment or to see the unity of the world of which I am a fragment. Genius is this seeing the unity of the world. It is a goal which brings meaning.

CHAPTER SEVEN

Historical determination of problems

Psychoanalysis is a system of thinking inserted into a particular historical niche. Does this mean that now that this piece of history is over, that psychoanalysis is over also? I think the answer to this question lies along the following lines. Freud was a genius and like all geniuses he was rooted in the emotional problem of his time and also in the thought fashion of his time and yet he transcended it. A genius always transcends his contemporaneous time slot.

What has to be done by the successors of a genius is to isolate the transcendent aspect, detach it from its historical time slot and then insert it into the social customs of our own contemporary period. What is necessary is to reach down to the essence of the process and thus to explore carefully to see what psychoanalysis really is. The philosopher, Alfred North Whitehead, said: "It is a well-founded historical generalization, that the last thing to be discovered in any science is what the science is really about" (1958, p. 167).

Simply speaking the problem that Freud met in his patients was the repression of their sexual desires. It was a problem in those patients of his but also this problem characterised that particular era in western Europe and the New World. Sex was something dirty; men were superior to women; homosexuality was a perversion and in most societies a criminal act. So sexual desires had to be suppressed and Freud had the view that a condemned sexual desire found expression in a piece of behaviour which was neurotic. Neurosis was the product of a dammed up sexual impulse that was forced to find expression in a different mode. This was his early theory but, as we saw in the last chapter, he changed from this position to one where the cause of neurosis became those incoherent parts of the personality which, because they were incoherent, were not conscious. Part of the problem, however, is that the early theory is the one which has most currency within the popular mind, but aspects of it also predominate among psychoanalysts and also in psychoanalytic institutes. I shall try in this chapter to find the essential aspect of Freud's theory but I know, because every theory is so embedded in the historical epoch some of which is still current today, that the result will be, must be, imperfect.

Freud's later theory is where he sees mental illness as being the manifestation of parts of the personality which are dissociated from the centre and therefore not coherent. Our view is that consciousness is the manifestation of what is coherent in the personality and unconsciousness discloses the presence of parts that are incoherent. Coherence comes about through an *all-inclusive principle* which binds them together. For coherence to extend its empire, so to speak, to include those elements outside the perimeter of its influence, a new principle needs to be discovered; a principle that is deeper, more abstract, that is capable of including within its structure not only those elements which, at the moment, are coherent but also those parts of the personality which are dissociated from the coherence of the centre. This means a demolition of that which is coherent because the renewed principle will reorder not only the elements which are incoherent but also those which are coherent. A new pattern will be necessary to incorporate the old and the new.

Once one gets outside this particular cultural time slot in which Freud found himself, one finds that sexuality was not repressed. So when Louis XIII of France was a baby of one year old and visitors came, male or female, they lifted his robe to look at his penis. Sometimes they tickled it with a feather or made jokes about it. There was no inhibition about talking of sex to children or touching their genitals (Aries, 1962, pp. 98–100). Louis XIII was born in 1601 so in the early part of the seventeenth century sex was part of everyday discourse even in the most aristocratic circles. This had changed fifty years later. I do not know quite why it had changed though I think it must be that Calvinism and the Puritan revolution of the sixteenth century was beginning to permeate the court life in France, London, and St. Petersburg. Calvin died in 1564—thirty-seven years before the birth of Louis XIII. But it seems that the severity of Calvin's hatred of sex took time before it infected the aristocracy of France through the spread of Huguenot influence. The Huguenots were a very influential minority in France. The Synod of Paris in 1559 consolidated the doctrines of Calvin among the Protestants in France. To begin with, the anti-sex attitude stayed within the Protestant realm but then through the spead of Jansenism it penetrated deeply into the Catholic Church but most particularly in France. As Calvinism spread via John Knox to Scotland and, at the same time, through Germany and into Austria, so to Freud. This puritanism never penetrated into Judaism and Freud may have benefited from this protective barrier. I sense also that this puritan attitude bloomed more profusely in aristocratic circles and that it never penetrated so deeply into the peasantry. It is significant that psychoanalysis found its home-land in middle class urban society. Although in France Louis XIV tried to reverse this trend yet it remained in place in western Europe and was solidly established at the time when Freud was investigating neurosis in the last decade of the nineteenth century. And in Victorian England prudery coloured the age whereas in India and China the sexual aspect of life was admired and paraded as can be seen from the sculptures at Khajuraho or in a reading of the Kama Sutra. The repression of sexual-ity as the cause of neurosis is a feasible proposition only in a limited historical time slot in one niche of our cultural world. It looks as though the factor that causes mental illness is not repression of sex but rather repression of any significant aspect of human life. In the time of Freud it was sex which was repressed. Today we repress racial hatred, distaste for homosexuality, and patriarchal attitudes. At a deeper level I believe that what is repressed is the personal. So Freud was right in his belief that repression of one part of the personality causes mental illness but was wrong in believing that this is was necessarily sex. Jung says that Freud was one-eyed in his insistence that the repression of sex was the cause of neurosis:

> I can still recall vividly how Freud said to me, 'My dear Jung, promise me never to abandon the sexual theory. That is the most essential thing of all. You see, we must make a dogma of it, an unshakable bulwark. (1977, p. 173)

Freud focused upon sex because repression of sexual desire was the fashion of his time though even here Sulloway has pointed out that there was much greater awareness of the sexuality of children in the last quarter of the nineteenth century than is normally acknowledged by those who champion Freud.

Freud's great contribution was to recognise that repression of something in the personality is the cause of mental illness. He observed correctly that the sexual was repressed in the social world in which he lived. He speaks about the way the sexual was repressed very clearly:

> There was some consolation for the bad reception accorded to my contention of a sexual aetiology in the neuroses even by my more intimate circle of friends—for a vacuum rapidly formed itself about my person—in the thought that I was taking up the fight for a new and original idea. But, one day, certain memories gathered in my mind which disturbed this pleasing notion, but which gave me in exchange a valuable insight into the processes of human creative activity and the nature of human knowledge. The idea for which I was being made responsible had by no means originated with me. It had been imparted to me by three people whose opinion had commanded my deepest respect—by Breuer himself, by Charcot, and by Chrobak, the gynaecologist at the University, perhaps the most eminent of all our Vienna physicians. These three men had all communicated to me a piece of knowledge which, strictly speaking, they themselves did not possess. Two of them later denied having done so when I reminded them of the fact; the third (the great Charcot) would probably have done the same if it had been granted me to see him again. But these three identical opinions, which I had heard without understanding, had laid dormant in my mind for years, until one day they awoke in the form of an apparently original discovery.
>
> One day, when I was a young house-physician, I was walking across the town with Breuer, when a man came up who evidently wanted to speak to him urgently. I fell behind. As soon as Breuer was free, he told me in his friendly, instructive way that this man was the husband of a patient of his and had brought him some news of her. The wife, he added, was behaving in such a peculiar way in society that she had been brought to him for treatment as a nervous case.

He concluded: "These things are always *secrets d'alcove!*" I asked him in astonishment what he meant, and he answered by explaining the word *alcove* (marriage-bed) to me, for he failed to realize how extraordinary the matter of his statement seemed to me.

Some years later, at one of Charcot's evening receptions, I happened to be standing near the great teacher at a moment when he appeared to be telling Brouardel a very interesting story about something that had happened during his day's work. I hardly heard the beginning, but gradually my attention was seized by what he was talking of: a young married couple from a distant country in the East—the woman a severe sufferer, the man either impotent or exceedingly awkward. "Tachez donc," I heard Charcot repeating, "je vous assure, vous y arriverez." Brouardel, who spoke less loudly, must have expressed his astonishment that symptoms like the wife's could have been produced by such circumstances. For Charcot suddenly broke out with great animation: "Mais, dans des cas pareils c'est toujours la chose génitale, toujours ... toujours ... toujours"; and he crossed his arms over his stomach, hugging himself and jumping up and down on his toes several times in his own characteristically lively way. I know that for a moment I was almost paralysed with amazement and said to myself: "Well, but if he knows that, why does he never say so?" But the impression was soon forgotten; brain anatomy and the experimental induction of hysterical paralyses absorbed all my interest.

A year later, I had begun my medical career in Vienna as a lecturer in nervous diseases, and in everything relating to the aetiology of the neuroses I was still as ignorant and innocent as one could expect of a promising student trained at a university. One day I had a friendly message from Chrobak, asking me to take a woman patient of his to whom he could not give enough time, owing to his new appointment as a university teacher. I arrived at the patient's house before he did and found that she was suffering from attacks of meaningless anxiety, and could only be soothed by the most precise information about where her doctor was at every moment of the day. When Chrobak arrived he took me aside and told me that the patient's anxiety was due to the fact that although she had been married for eighteen years she was still *virgo intacta*. The husband was absolutely impotent. In such cases, he said, there was nothing for a medical man to do but to shield this domestic misfortune with his own reputation, and put up with it if people shrugged their shoulders and said of him: "He's no good if he can't cure her after so many years." The sole prescription for such a malady, he added, is familiar enough to us, but we cannot order it. It runs: "*R. Penis normalis dosim repetatur!*" I had never heard of such a prescription, and felt inclined to shake my head over my kind friend's cynicism.

I have not of course disclosed the illustrious parentage of this scandalous idea in order to saddle other people with the responsibility for it. I am well aware that it is one thing to give utterance to an idea once or twice in the form of a passing *aperçu*, and quite another to mean it seriously—to take it literally and pursue it in the face of every contradictory detail, and to win it a place among accepted truths. It is the difference between a casual flirtation and a legal marriage with all its duties and difficulties. (Freud, 1914d, pp. 12–15)

So Freud had seen clearly the way in which the sexual was privately known but not acknowledged publicly and scientifically. Freud's mistake was to believe that this was a permanent cause of neurosis. One would expect a lesser thinker to make this mistake but it is surprising with his erudition and historical knowledge that he did not revise his opinion, but this is only testament to my own tendency to place great thinkers on a pedestal way above our own level. Great thinkers have blind spots. They can have huge insight in one domain and yet be blind in another. It is particularly important that we see the blind spots in great thinkers because, in admiration of their genius, it is easy to dismiss them. It is more important to see and publish the blind spots of great thinkers because the error can be shielded behind the great thinker's fame. I think that Jung correctly sensed that Freud was too narrowly focused upon the sexual to the exclusion of other factors. He was not able to let historical knowledge open his mind to other domains of experience which had been repressed in previous eras. Had he been able to do so then he would have put all the weight of his mind and authority behind repression as the agent causing neurosis. The sexual was something that was only repressed within quite a limited time slot in European history; but repression of *something* in the personality has been and is present in every culture. If the repression of this *something* is the cause of mental illness then Freud came up with a revolutionary insight, and I believe he did. The fact that his focus limited it to the sphere of sexuality is a social disaster. So mental illness occurs when something elemental to the human make-up is repressed.

There are certain factors in the personality that are essential to human functioning. I am going to omit the physiological ones like hearing, sight, and touch, not because these are not crucial but because they are well known, and instead attend to the essential psychological factors. I put first perception. Sensations—visual, auditory, and tactile—bombard the organism; the capacity to receive, select, and arrange them is called perception. There are two ways in which perception may be functioning badly. Any one of these sub-factors may be undeveloped or these three sub-factors may not be in the right relation to one another. Just as attachment of one individual to another may be of a clinging or symbolic kind so also the relation of parts within the self can be in either of these two modes. Now, perception may be undeveloped. In psychoanalytic discourse the term *infantile* is often used. The *infantile transference* is a term used to mean that the whole personality is in a state of dependence upon the other. But this needs to be understood in the following way. One part of the personality is undeveloped. For the sake of argument let us say that it is the capacity to arrange the received sensations in an ordered pattern. When this capacity is unknown, it affects the whole personality. Rather than know that this capacity to order the received sensations is undeveloped it is preferable to criticise harshly the whole system. This camouflages the particular function which is still in a baby state. Shame hides this baby; there is no star of Bethlehem here.

Perception, along with cognition and motivation, is one of the basic topics in any psychology course. It is concerned with the registration within the organism of the material world around us. It registers phenomena but not the noumenon. There is, however, a faculty that does register the noumenon. This is what the scholastic philosophers called the intellect; intellect, not intelligence. It is the intellect that grasps being. It is the faculty of the real. This also can be undeveloped. It can be undeveloped through genetic inheritance or through lack of practice. The intellect not only grasps being itself but also the principles that unify diverse modes of operation in the world of the senses. So, for instance, volume, weight, and density are such unifying principles. Each of these entities is in the phenomenal world but they are not grasped through perception but through the intellect. So intellect also can either be well developed or in an undeveloped state.

This way in which any one of us can exclude a particular faculty is not confined to the individual. Historical epochs as well as particular disciplines within a defined slot of history exclude from their vision particular portions of human functioning. No one has given more potent expression to this than Paul Tillich:

> Our period has become what it is through innumerable decisions and, therefore, innumerable exclusions. Some of the excluded possibilities have died away, depriving us of their creative power … At the beginning of our period we decided for freedom. It was a right decision; it created something new and great in history. But in that decision we excluded the security, social and spiritual, without which man cannot live and grow. And now, in the old age of our period, the quest to sacrifice freedom for security splits every nation and whole world with really daemonic power. (1964b, pp. 179–180)

In our era, within the discipline of psychoanalysis inner freedom of choice has been excluded in favour of two seeming contraries: determinism and intentionality. We humans are the pawns of instinctual forces and outer stimuli and are deprived of any inner freedom of choice: thus speaks the determinist philosophy; it is my fault that this baby died, it is my fault that my son has become an alcoholic, it is my fault that Mr Smith is director of my corporation because I encouraged his ambitions when he was yet a junior. This is the intentional philosophy. Now, these two are coupled in an inseparable embrace but how is this? How can this be so when they seem on the surface to be in direct contradiction to each other? The clue lies in the phrase *on the surface*. In each case too great a weight is being put upon, first, the non-personal elements in the personality and, second, the personal elements. There is a deeper factor being excluded: *acceptance*. Acceptance of what is. Intentionality can be defined as a focus upon the other. What I do to the other becomes the focus of attention. The problem however is that this is then defined by the individual who is wounded by the other. The pain that I suffer is given the attribution of a bad intention on the part of the other. It is a morality based upon what I suffer, not what I do. This is the case of bad intentionality, but what about good intentionality? This also gets perverted into that which pleases me, gives me pleasure, makes me happy. Intentionality then is rooted in the hedonistic philosophy.

> There is a powerful movement of critical thought that has been a
> work to eliminate any quest for an understanding that carries with
> it the metaphysical implications of a groping for reality behind a
> screen of appearances … Our acknowledgment of understanding
> as a valid form of knowing will go a long way towards liberating
> our minds from this violent and inefficient despotism. (Polanyi,
> 1959, pp. 20–21)

There is a deep kindness in acceptance; there is a cruelty in a selection which excludes one's essential being. Acceptance honours the complexity of factors. Determinism is closely allied with the hedonistic principle and this means that determinism endorses an intentionality that is concerned with what gives me pleasure or pain. This shuts out one's essential being and whenever something is shut out like this it comes back and bites us with a daemonic power. Acceptance of both is what endows the human condition with a favoured kindness.

These twin principles—determinism and intentionality—as a system shut out the courageous, the formative, the noble. See for instance the view of Macneile Dixon:

> To our preposterous race obstacles are the breath of life. It turns
> wearily and dejectedly away from the easy and the obvious, and
> delights in its objects and its pains. If you would make human
> beings happy, give them a task and a cause, and the harder the
> better. They rise to their full stature only when challenged. Startle
> the soul into admiration, ask of it the impossible, to join the forlorn
> hope, and it is endowed with angelic strength. Ask nothing of it
> and the soul retires. (1958, p. 228)

This is a view opposite to the one that says what humans most ardently seek is the avoidance of pain and the experience of pleasure. We are not determined by something but going towards something. This is elemental to life. It is what distinguishes a living thing from a dead piece of matter. The living thing gropes towards. It has an end beyond itself. Bergson defined life as the *tendency to act on matter* which emphasises the object towards which life tends, and Streeter held that life embodies its own cause, which stresses the source of living things.

> In the study of living organisms all that we can observe is behaviour, that is, a series of motions and reactions which take place after the impact or apposition of other bodies or forces to which we give the name "stimuli". So much can we observe; what then is it that we infer? We infer that these motions and reactions are accompanied by, and are the resultants of the presence in the organism of the thing we call "life". Moreover, we say at once of certain types of motion and reaction that they are, and of certain others that they are not, a sign of the presence of life. The word life, then, differs from words like "oscillation" or "rebound" in that it is not a name that we bestow on a particular type of motion or reaction; it is a cause which we assume to be capable of accounting for them. More than that, it is not a cause assumed to exist, though in itself unknown; it is not some hypothetical entity which might just as well be called x; it is something the nature of which is taken for granted to be a matter of familiar knowledge. (Streeter, 1935, pp. 98–99)

We have to try to get some purchase on what we mean by the noble. It must be something to do with acting towards something which is beyond our own comfort zone. There is a sense when one speaks of someone acting for a noble cause that she acts for something which is beyond self-interest; that she puts her own individual needs in second place. This way of talking suggests that she puts something else first. This something else is not the other person to the exclusion of all else. Even a mother who concentrates all her energy on the care of her sick child is doing something more than doing everything for this child. She is ministering to something that is beyond herself. This child will outlive her. One of the greatest sadnesses is for a mother or a father to live to see their own child die. The next generation is something beyond. The mother might say, "There is something more valuable than my own individual existence." There is a judgment that there is something of value which is beyond, higher, deeper than what appears on the surface. My own needs for food, for sexual satisfaction, for drink, for shelter, are secondary to something more essential. There is being, the reality of things which cannot be seen, heard, or touched but is known through an act of the mind, an act of the intellect. I am using the word "intellect" as it was used by Thomas Aquinas and the Scholastics. It referred to a separate faculty that grasped existence itself. The only trouble with this word is that it conjures up an object which is static. The imagery behind "existence" is static, though if one abstracts existence not from the inanimate world but from life then one gets a sense of a burgeoning embryo of creative energy. The essence of life is that it creates beyond its own circumference. The mammal creates a new being. It is definitely on life itself that one needs to concentrate one's attention. If the planet is tending towards life then it is through life itself that one looks for an understanding that is faithful to the essence of the universe. We tend to dismiss this because in the vastness of the universe astronomers have only recently found stars, other than the sun, with their own planets and at the moment life has not been found on them. If then we abstract from life rather than from inanimate nature, or rather see even inanimate nature as itself tending towards life, which has some confirmation from the discovery of DNA, then the world's substance in its very essence consists of a *towardness*.

Freud was also embedded in a system of thinking that tried to fit human beings into a natural philosophy that was mechanical. He studied under Brücke in his physiological laboratory in Vienna. Brücke, together with Helmholtz, Ludwig, and Du Bois-Reymond had, in 1842, signed the anti-vitalist pact in the following words:

> No other forces than the common physical and chemical ones are active within the organism. In those cases which cannot at the time be explained by those forces one has either to find the specific way or form of their action by means of the physical-mathematical method or to assume new forces equal in dignity to the chemical-physical forces inherent in matter, reducible to the force of attraction and repulsion. (Jones, 1972, p. 45)

In 1845 these four men formed a small private club called the *Berliner Physicalische Gesellschaft*. Freud espoused this mechanical model with a passion. It was this mechanism which inherently led to repression of the person. The person results from a life-creation. Determinism, which is the belief that all movement is due to the organism being pushed from outside, shut out vehemently any causal principle finding its origin entirely within the organism. So if Calvin was partly responsible for the repression of sex, Freud is partly responsible for the repression of the person. Freud emphasised that neurosis resulted from the repression of sexual impulses. What he did not see sufficiently clearly, however, was that repression of any element that was essential to the human condition led to mental illness. Each age represses some crucial aspect of the human condition, so therefore the mental illness of one age differs from that of another according to what is repressed. Repression of the person leads to a different kind of mental illness to repression of sex. Each age is characterised by its own form of mental illness.

The mental illness which Freud encountered was that which arose from the repression of sex and he rightly recognised this and developed a method to undo it. But the characteristic of this age is not the repression of sex but the repression of the person. This is not quite the right way to think about it. If we make an historical survey of any particular human feature we will find that a repression has always existed but it reaches a crescendo where human beings become intolerant of it. So the person has always been a casualty of those great tides of historical imperatives but it has reached such a proportion in this age that patients come to therapists crying against this tyrannical imposition. "We are persons," they cry, "and we want to take possession of our birthright."

This implies that there is a knowledge of that which is repressed but it is not a knowledge with a definite outline. We cannot see its silhouette. We know that which is not there. We need to reflect upon what is meant by repression. Words can be revealers but also deceivers. The word "repression" conjures up a something which is being pushed down but this imagery is wrong. Freud says at one point that repression is the removal of attention. Attention, like recognition, is a psychic mode which brings that which it attends to into existence. Attention is a fertilising act. Remove attention and the potential being does not come to birth.

Again and again in the consulting room of the psychotherapist and psychoanalyst the cry comes forth from the patient, trying to describe her frustration, that her parents fed her, looked after her health, made sure her teeth were fine, made sure she went to a good school, supported her financially through university but—and here is the centre of her complaint—but … they did not know *me*. When, in a particular epoch, a crucial factor in the human make-up is being crushed, then a cry starts to be heard. So, when sexual desire is being suppressed severely and with a continuity which it seems would never end within a particular culture then a cry goes up, usually from one small group gathered around a particular individual. It is like the cry of a group of supporters on behalf of an unfairly imprisoned man. Freud and his early circle of admirers cried out against the cruel oppression of sexuality.

"Look", they said, "at the neurotic suffering that this suppression is causing," and they set about devising a therapeutic method to release these victims from their plight. We can say that Freud's cry has been largely successful. In Western culture people give much greater expression to their sexual desire than they did before Freud's day. There has been a revolution in sexual mores. Homosexuality has been decriminalised in nearly all societies; sex outside marriage is no longer frowned upon. The taboo that remains is sex with children or incestuous relations. Although a lot needs to be achieved still in order to define more clearly what is a healthy sexuality, yet Freud's clamour has achieved its aim and some of the neurotic phenomena associated with this repression have almost disappeared: hysterical conversion for instance.

This absence in the cry of the individual in the psychotherapist's consulting room is paralleled in the cry coming from society as a whole.

For Freud the agent of repression was the superego which was the seat of the death instinct. Today the repressing agency remains the super ego but rather than being the seat of the death instinct it is the representative abode of society. Society is compressed within the personality as the super ego.

The savage superego is a monster within, which is the mind's way of representing an absence. So the monster tells me: "See, you're useless, you're hopeless, you don't deserve to exist." That is the way the monster carries on, but really it points to an absence within or to an undeveloped function, and because the mind cannot represent an absence it constructs a monster. And therefore in my view, I do not think I would have a practice if no people had a powerful superego. The consulting rooms are full of people with powerful superegos.

Society's aim through the agency of the superego is to mould the personality according to the social template. Talcott Parsons expanded the concept of the superego to include this social dimension:

> ... the place of the superego as part of the structure of the personality must be understood in terms of the relation between personality and the total common culture, by virtue of which a stable system of social interaction on the human levels becomes possible. Freud's insight was profoundly correct when he focused on the element of moral standards. This is, indeed, central and crucial, but it does seem that Freud's view was too narrow.

> The inescapable conclusion is that not only moral standards, but *all the components of the common culture* are internalized as part of the personality structure. (1970, p. 23)

Because what is internalised is the common culture it has a huge power as the individual yearns to be freed of isolation. There are two ways out of this isolation: either the individual accomodates himself to the social norm and thus acquires a feeling of togetherness with the group. This helps to dilute the pain of isolation. It does not, however, resolve it. The resolution of isolation cannot be achieved through accommodation of this kind because it is based on an attachment which occurs at the surface of the personality. Liberation from isolation is only possible through a connection to another or others from the centre of the personality and not through a surface attachment to others.

The creative centre, the creative principle, is in its nature *in-relation*. This is its nature. What is required of the individual is to let go of "sense-attachment" and fall back upon his inner core, this creative principle, which is *in-relation*. Isolation is overcome through being connected to my inner being.

This creative principle which is *in-relation* is what defines the person. The person is *in-relation* to the other and also inwardly connected within the self. The interpersonal and the intrapsychic are two aspects of one thing.

It is this creative centre which is repressed by the social pressure that has arisen from beliefs dominating society at present.

CHAPTER EIGHT

Resistance to becoming a person

To the extent to which I am a person I suffer shame, guilt, disappointment, sadness, regret, envy, and jealousy. I also become capable of love, gratitude, generosity, forgiveness, and magnanimity, and am capable of experiencing joy, beauty, and happiness. I also experience tragedy.

Becoming a person puts a demand upon me in two different directions:

Pain and turbulence

I come to know tragedy and this is an agony. I will certainly experience a turbulence, I will go through an inner torture. I emphasise the word *feel* because these realities are there prior to the individual becoming a person but they are not felt. So how do they exist in the untransformed state? When something is felt it has been embraced within the personality; it has been loved; it is united through the *all-inclusive principle* to other elements in the personality. So in the untransformed state it is hated, is discharged out of the personality into the body, into sexual behaviour, into social conduct, or into an ideology.

What quite do we mean when we say that it is "discharged out of the personality"? One concurrent phenomenon is that the *I* is dead. It is wooden; the *I* is programmed like a robot. It is in reactive mode. So a man asked me, "Neville, tell me, am I happy?" What we are saying is that the element cannot be ejected from the personality but the personality can be deadened or prevented from coming into life. A man's mother abused his girlfriend so he married in reaction to his mother's action. There is a living emotional principle that gives life to the elements in the personality. It is like the heart which pumps blood out through the arteries and from the arteries into the arterioles to every part of the body. It reaches all areas. When something painful has happened it resists the blood coming to it. A resistance can be so great that it prevents the heart pumping at all.

The question though is: does a dead element function in the personality?, and the answer is that it functions in the same way as any piece of inanimate matter functions. It moves in the personality by the same principle as any piece of inanimate matter moves. A rock rolls down a hill and collides with a stone which, in its turn, starts rolling down the hill. The stimulus-response theory of motivation finds its origin in an innovator who is an amorphous human being. The stimulus-response view of the behavioural psychologist has to be overthrown. And this view is not restricted to CBT. This is the belief that the human organism is entirely shaped by the stimuli that bombard it.

I need to explain what I mean by an "amorphous human being". I could have said an "individual" because this is different from a person but I want to make quite sure here that a person is differentiated from a somebody who is not a person. As long as "individual" is understood as an "amorphous human being" and not a person then that is fine. What I want to stress is that the hated elements inside me cannot be discharged into a person. A person is one who has embraced the elements through the agency of an inner emotional principle so there is a oneness guided from within; a foreign body being discharged from the outside just cannot enter because of the inner coherence. You can throw a stone at a rubber statue and it will bounce off it; it cannot enter it. I am born as a mass of disparate elements; I become a person at the moment when these come together into a unity through an inner mental principle. I referred in Chapter Four to an *all-inclusive principle*. This is a mental principle which includes all the disparate elements and does not exclude any. Truth, love, trust are such principles. When there is a coherence generated by such a mental principle then I cannot be broken up by the group mass.

We must look into the reason for the hatred. There is something in me that is not known, that is unfamiliar. The hatred is the emotional consequence of meeting something which is alien. The need to know is my security blanket. Knowing something is the consequence of coming into relation with it. I come into relation with it through participation. There is a sameness between myself and the thing known. And the question here is, what is this sameness? What is the sameness between myself and a star, between myself and a crocodile, between myself and a daisy, between myself and Caesar, between myself and Hitler, between myself and Churchill, between myself and Mother Teresa?

Clearly there is a greater sameness between me and Caesar than between me and a stone. One way of making a hierarchy of sameness is to place Pure Being at the top of the schedule and then at the bottom the greatest quantum of non-being. Non-being is a difficult concept to grasp. We can only get at it through an analysis of Being of which non-being is the negative. Pure Being just *is*. The essential point is that this sameness, this oneness, is the essence of all various things and therefore is respectful of them.

This sameness is something that I can capture in the numerous variations within the contours of my own daily mental life. I like to think of myself as stable, steady, and always in balance, but in fact I am a living being and the emotional variety of what happens inside me is as vast as the changing landscape during a storm. The idea that the right thing is always to be in balance finds support in W. B. Cannon's theory of *homeostasis*. The homeostatic theory had a forerunner in Fechner's *theory of constancy* which Freud adopted and used as the principle governing the *modus operandi* of the instincts.

Yesterday I went into a shop and the young girl serving me had a silver pinhead button planted in her nose. I did not like it and wanted to alienate myself from someone with such a taste in bodily decorative art. It indicates a something in myself that I do not know. It is there but I do not know it. It is unfamiliar; it frightens me. What is it in myself that I cringe away from? I would not have cringed in that way if I had observed that she was wearing earrings? When I saw her I remembered that my elder son wore an earring for a short time. I did not like it but I also had the thought when I was in that shop that it was a good thing that I was able, though with difficulty, to tolerate his wearing of an earring. I said to myself, "It is much better that he has tried it and found for himself that he does not want to wear it or that it does not 'fit' for him." How is he truly to know what is right for him unless he tries it? But, had he decided that it was right for him I believe that I would have accepted that. So, in that ninety seconds while I was waiting at the counter for the lady with the nose-button to serve me, my mind was in turbulence: it started with hatred, then a reflection leading to a memory which had in it my emotional attitude from when my son first decided to wear an earring to my own considered judgment when he had finished, followed by my further thought that he being who he is, and finding that through his own discovery, is what was most important for me. So the ninety seconds ended with making contact with a mental principle that is central for me. And the trajectory of my mind in those ninety seconds was a line which went up and down the graph in great peaks and troughs.

The beckoning towards love

An inner beckoning towards love, towards gratitude, towards generosity, towards forgiveness and magnanimity—this redirecting of my inner self and a pulling away from habit, a pulling away from what is familiar— causes turbulence, like the ferment that occurs when the sodium and chlorine molecules fuse into a new compound that we call salt.

Love opens the personality to the ultimate whereas hatred focuses it in, upon a target that is narrower than itself. The focus of hatred is always upon a fragment of the whole but in such a way that the entirety of the whole is shut out. This is epitomised in obsessional neurosis where the mind is engaged in a worrying way upon a fragment, the effect of which is to shut out the immensity of reality itself. It therefore closes the individual to the wider horizon. The more intense the focus the more of the totality of the real is pushed out. This is so if the target of the focus is a sensual object or fact. Targeting such an object shuts out all other objects in the field. One sensual object cuts out another—a focus on one shuts out the other. Like the vase or two faces—if you look at one you shut out the other and vice versa. This is why the focus always needs to be upon a mental principle that I have called an *all-inclusive principle* which, unlike a sensual object, embraces all the variety within it. I can *know* that the vase and two faces are present but cannot see it through my eyes that way. The knowledge here is of a something that is devoid of the sensual component arrived at through sight. But what is this something? Plato, I believe, was trying to get at this when he proposed the eternal forms. It is a mental principle. I can know *it*. Love therefore is the emotion whose goal is an *all-inclusive principle*, so in this case the vase and the two faces are known. Hatred, on the other hand, is the emotion whose focus is a sensual object. This hatred is therefore derived from the sensual whereas love is derived from a mental principle.

This sensual object can be either outside or inside the personality. The focus is upon something that has happened to the personality and this is sensual in nature and is either avoided because it is painful or cherished because it is pleasurable; its pleasure or unpleasure is registered through the senses. If it is an outer thing like a cup of coffee it is experienced as pleasurable if it stimulates a pleasure centre in the brain; if the coffee is too hot and it burns the tongue then unpleasure is registered. More relevant though is an event that has happened to someone. Let us take an historical example. At the beginning of the First World War Churchill was First Lord of the Admiralty. In this position he devised the plan to send a fleet through the Dardanelles, capture Constantinople, link up with the Russian army and, with this combined strength, to defeat the German army in Europe. However, the venture failed because the Admiral of the Fleet lost his nerve when three ships were sunk in the narrows before reaching the Sea of Marmara. Churchill then was the whipping boy and was the scapegoat for this failure. So here was the event. He could have let it destroy him. But, in a letter to his wife in December 1915, he said: "As one's fortunes are reduced, one's spirit must expand to fill the void" (Soames, 1999, p. 139).

This is a better example than the one of a cup of coffee spilling over one, burning one's tongue. It is a painful event within the individual's personal history but the personality can either focus in upon it with hatred or place it within an ultimate: embracing a look forward to a future beyond. This ultimate can be Being itself but there are representations of Being that are greater than the wound to the self. These might be thought of as the characters of Being. These are goodness, freedom, and personal relating. All the greats of history like Shakespeare, Tolstoy, Gandhi, Churchill, or Mandela have been guided by these ultimate principles to which family, tribal, or national belonging come second. These characteristics of Being which are already inherent within the personality put a demand upon the personality to open out to them.

This expansion of the personality to these essences of Being is what is called love. This love expands the personality. The personality is affected by the goal towards which it relates and with which it participates. If it shares in the wide horizons of Being itself, it expands; if it clings to its own wounds it shrinks. This way of considering the personality chimes with Bion's principle that the aim of psychoanalysis is the development of the personality. The unpleasure of his fortunes being reduced was not Churchill's focus but rather a demand from the ultimate that his spirit had to expand to fill the void.

But this pleasure or unpleasure centre becomes the focus of all attention. This is the consequence of an emotional wound so that all attention is upon what has happened to me. What the *I does* in its reach towards reality is totally shut out. There is a need in the process of collecting data to focus upon the assembled facts and then remove the mind to the ultimate and back so that there is a constant nourishment of the one by the other. If the ultimate alone is focused upon, then the datum of experience will be forced into an *a priori* mode. The datum of experience has to be *seen through* to the mental principle that represents it rather than have what has been perceived thrust into a mould in which it does not fit. There is a hierarchy of ideas from most to least abstract. Being itself is not an idea but the real. Ideas then represent the mental principles that link the data of experience. They are an intermediate between facts as sensed and Being itself. How does the mind get from the sensual datum to the mental principle and from there to the ultimate? This first step is extremely mysterious but it must, I believe, be that there is a sympathy of similarity between these mental principles and the mind, so that when the similarity reaches a closeness then the mind does make this leap from one to the other, or at least that it can, because the realisations of an Archimedes or a Newton demonstrate it; but how their minds made that leap from the sensual object or objects to the mental principle is an unknown at this stage in the development of our brains.[1] The step from there to a realisation of the ultimate is achieved differently. We are here connecting to reality and not an idea and this is achieved through a personal act of understanding. However, as Being is the substance of all that there is in all its variety, there is a grasp of things in their entirety. In this sense, but this alone, there is a similarity between the ultimate and mental principles. They both penetrate realities without destroying their nature because they are an elemental part of their nature.

When the sensual object is extremely focused in upon, then just the present moment with the self as a wounded object fills the whole mental screen. Paranoia is my registration of the fact that I am not free.

All other objects are shut out including the past and future. These are totally obliterated. This can be observed when a patient is entirely dominated by the impact of the present moment in the consulting room. Yesterday and tomorrow are non-existent. Sometimes, reinforced by theoretical justifications, the analyst is also in this mode. This intense focus is when there has been a wound to the self. This may have been thirty years before but it has remained as a solid object within the personality, revealing itself in physical illness, fanatical attachment to an ideology or its icon, to hatred of individuals and groups.

The past and the future require some element of the *all-inclusive principle* to be able to be encompassed. To the extent that this is absent, differences are obliterated with the result that separate entities become coalesced into one amorphous mass. This is because all has to be crammed into the focused fragment. Differences require a judging capacity which is a faculty that is outside the immediate sense experience. We see this clearly in an obsession where someone is focused in upon one object of a sensual kind that necessarily shuts out other objects. This fits with Freud's view that repression consists in the removal of attention from an object. So it is removed from the place liable to cause the greatest guilt, shame, regret, or sadness and transferred to something trivial. However, what Freud's description does not encompass is the mental principle, so when he talks of the withdrawal of a cathexis of energy it is correct in that the particular datum is no longer known, but he does not say to where that cathexis of energy is now removed. He clearly must see that the cathexis is removed to another object, but the idea that it could be removed to a mental principle which includes the original object and the new one is absent from his thinking. The place that causes such pain is always the totality. Bléandonu quotes Bion as saying, "In the last analysis he defines the psychotic part of the personality as a tendency to aim at the destruction of all functions of unification ..." (1994, p. 136).

It is seeing the totality that opens one to tragedy and the follies of human existence—one's own as well as others'.

It is a natural instinct in all animals, including the human animal, to avoid pain. But the price of becoming a person is that the pains of life, past, present, and future have to be embraced. It is the cost of becoming a person. Embracing pain is not driven by a masochistic orgy but because pain is part of living, and if one is to engage with life then it is not possible to do so while leaving the pain on one side. If I attempt to embrace life while excluding pain then I remain on the outside. Again, Wilfred Bion (1963) says:

> Pain cannot be absent from the personality. An analysis must be painful, not because there is necessarily any value in pain, but because an analysis in which pain is not observed and discussed cannot be regarded as dealing with one of the central reasons for the patient's presence. (1989, p. 61)

Becoming a person opens the personality to the torture of guilt. There are two actions that characterise the human being's relation to the world—centripetal and centrifugal. You do not have to be a person in order to experience the centripetal stimuli but as the centrifugal ones issue from the agent at the centre you have to be a person in order to experience them. It is the person who experiences those actions that have a moral dimension. It is important to note that the word "experience" does not refer just to feelings but also to knowledge. Knowledge through inference is also part of our experience.

There are motor activities which are morally neutral. There are emotional activities which have a moral bearing. Love embraces the elements in the personality, creating them into a newborn unity. Hatred discharges these elements out of the personality. They may be discharged into the body, into sexual activity, into speech, into an *imago*, into an amorphous human being, into an ideology. But they stay there as bits that trap the personality. They trap the personality because the individual becomes subject to them; the personality is dominated by them. So, for instance, when it is discharged into the sexual arena then the personality is forced to act according to the demand of this part. This is because all parts belong to the whole and there is a magnetic attraction between the whole and a discharged part, whereas when a part is embraced within the *all-inclusive principle* then there is a free relation between parts rather than a magnetism that cannot be resisted.

There are two ways in which one human can connect to another. One has to think of the individual made up of two components: Being and non-being. *In-relation* is a property of Being. What I have referred to above as the "sensual" is *non-being* (Tillich, 1964a, p. 41ff).

In *non-being* there is no relation so there is just an agglomerated mass. In an agglomeration there is no intrinsic relation between one thing and another. *Non-being* has no relational property and because of this one thing is stuck to another; they are not in relation to one another. What I have just described of human individuals is also so of the elements inside any one individual. They either stick to each other magnetically or are in relation. *In-relation* is a property of Being; love is the *in-relation* property of Being. Hatred is *non-relation*, is *non-being* so the personality is stuck to the part that is hated. It is not in relation to it but instead is slave to it. This shuts out tragedy which requires the bird's eye view of the human condition. We can only become a person if we embrace the tragic. Essentially the tragic is the human attempt to side-step the inevitable, to shut out fate, to attempt to avoid what cannot be avoided. There are several dimensions to the tragic which we need now to consider.

The first concerns the limitations of myself. I was born. This was something concerning which I had no choice. I was born to a particular set of parents; I was born in a particular country; I was born into a particular social class; I was born at a particular moment in the history of the human race on the planet Earth. These are the facts. Now, as I wrote in Chapter Three, these can be the object of a creation but we can only create from facts, these facts. One might say that they are dead facts. Under the creative act they become alive. When this creative act has not occurred then we are victim to these facts of our destiny rather than them being the subject of creative possibility. When the individual has not made this creative act then he or she walks in tragedy. People will see the individual as a tragic figure. The tragic is when the individual is not aware of these elements, this slime of the earth out of which he is fashioned. Such an individual is driven, like a dry leaf in the wind, by these cultural facts of which he is a part. If they are recognised it is because the creative power, as a property of Being, has been exercised upon them. Realisation is the signal that the creative act has occurred.

The other aspect of tragedy is that the individual is confronted with dilemmas that are beyond his emotional capacity to solve. The tragedy of Shakespeare's *Hamlet* has been interpreted in this sense. He was given the knowledge of his uncle's murder of his father but was unable to deal with it. As Tillich says: "For man is not equal to his own experience" (1964b, p. 54).

This formulation of Tillich's corresponds to Bion's (1963) model of container and contained. In this case the container cannot hold the content (the experience) (1984, p. 7). This was elementally so of Hamlet. One can think of the ghost of his father as Shakespeare's way of conveying an insight that Hamlet had into the real situation. Isaiah Berlin said of Vico that he did not have enough talent for his genius and mentions (1979, p. 114) that Heine noted that this was also true of Berlioz. The tragedy here is that the genius within the personality does not have the practical "talent" sufficient to deal with the genius within. One would need to dissect in each case, in Vico and Berlioz, what was that talent which they lacked. Hamlet did not have the emotional resources to solve the dilemma that his insight had put him in. Another way of thinking of this is to say that Hamlet had an insight but did not believe it. Belief is that psychological process whereby the whole personality is gathered into the creative insight. Hamlet's insight was creative but he saw into something which was intensely painful but it divided him. Something prevented him from bringing all elements of his personality under the guidance of that insight.

What is so within the individual is also true of the individual within the group. Again, Wilfred Bion addresses this problem in his chapter on the mystic and the group in *Attention and Interpretation*. Here it is no longer the genius not having the resources within the personality but rather the group not being equal to the insight of the individual genius.

> It would be surprising if any true mystic were not regarded by the group as a mystical nihilist at some stage of his career and by a greater or lesser proportion of the group. It would be equally surprising if he were not in fact nihilistic to some group if for no other reason than that the nature of his contribution is certain to be destructive of the laws, conventions, culture, and therefore coherence, of a group within the group, if not the whole group. (1970, p. 64)

This again is tragedy. Here the tragedy is experienced in the individual genius but also retrospectively in later years and, to quote Newman (1875), perhaps even five hundred years later. What would happen if the group were able to open itself and find the resources to measure up to the genius in their midst? Elemental to genius is direct experience of the social problem and the direction in which a solution is to be found. If the group opens itself to this vision within its midst it then has to abandon cherished ideals which protect it from direct experience. Direct contact means the personalities of the group have to start again, start from babyhood and this is painful.

What is so of the individual, of the group, is also so of the large cultural group where huge upheavals occur within history, with which humans are not able to deal until a genius appears on the scene. Political geniuses like King David, Julius Caesar, Francis Drake, Thomas Jefferson, Gandhi, Churchill, Lawrence of Arabia, Gorbachev, or Mandela have the insight to manage what the ordinary man is unable to do. Tragedy is when the event is greater than human minds are able to meet. The tragedy today (2008) in the Middle East is that there is no Churchill, Gandhi, or Mandela to solve the chaos. We look with great admiration to scientific geniuses in the natural sciences like Archimedes, Copernicus, Newton, Kepler, Darwin, or Einstein, or in the human sciences like Kierkegaard, Ruskin, Tolstoy, Freud, Jung, or Bion. In the arts we have Johann Sebastian Bach, Mozart, Giotto, Michelangelo, Raphael, El Greco, Cézanne, or Van Gogh. In literature we have Shakespeare, Dostoyevsky, Tolstoy, Jane Austen, Emily Brönte, or George Eliot. In religion we have the Buddha, Mahavira, Zarathustra, Isaiah, Jesus, St Augustine, Muhammad, Moses Maimonides, Thomas Aquinas, Luther, or Pope John XXIII. What we admire is that we see instances here of minds that were able to "meet" the problems confronting them at the time. Tragedy is that there have been so few of such human giants and that great periods of hopeless inability have to be suffered until a genius appears who is able to solve the problem of the age. It is the poverty of the human mind in the face of what it needs to solve. I mention here great figures but there have been also hidden or forgotten geniuses like Harrison who solved the problem of longitude (Sobel, 1998) or Vico who grasped the knowledge peculiar to interpersonal facts but this was only recognised by Michelet a hundred years after he had lived. John Henry Newman said wisely:

> He knows that present opinions are the accident of the day, and that they will fall as they have risen. They will surely fall even though at a distant date. He labours for that time; he labours for five hundred years to come. He can bear in faith to wait five hundred years, to wait for an era long, long after he has mouldered into dust. (1875, pp. 249–250)

One might refer to this as cultural tragedy but there is also what might be called evolutionary tragedy. The inability to solve a problem may be because the development of the brain has not been sufficient for the problem which needs to be solved. *Homo Erectus* with a brain size of 1000 c.c. was not able to represent or symbolise. Today with a brain size of 1450 c.c. we cannot solve problems which our descendants in two million years time with a brain size of 1700 c.c. will be able to solve. If, although oversimplifying, the mind has a more intricate instrument with more functions, then it will be able to solve greater problems.

The grasping of the limitations of the individual, the culture, and the evolutionary stage of development is something that occurs through a personal creative act. As Mary Warnock puts it in *Existentialism* (1979, p. 9), "… it cannot be passed on from one person to the next, nor added to by different researchers. It cannot be taught in the classroom." It is a creative act that fashions the person and in this act tragedy is inherently contained. This is because no one can make or determine a creative act. Its essential nature is that it springs totally from within and unexpectedly. There is an inner principle that has no outside cause. This is what defines life and has been well argued by Streeter as mentioned in the last chapter.

The creative act comes entirely from within although the right surrounding circumstances can favour it but not cause it. At each point in the fashioning of the person there is a confrontation with past regrets, knowledge of one's fate, a vision of the culture, and the sight of our evolutionary stage. All this is extremely painful and requires an opening of our minds and we have to leave behind treasured zones of comfort. There is then a resistance to becoming a person.

This is a power that lies at the heart of life. Lamarck it was who understood this in opposition to Georges Cuvier, his rival. Georges Cuvier found fossils of animals that no longer existed so he said that certain animals have become extinct. He was the first scientist to make that discovery. So one species of animal becomes extinct and then how does another come about? Cuvier insisted that it was through divine intervention. God bowed down to the world and created a new species. This might be called "periodic creationism" (Honeywill, 2008, pp. 39–44). Lamarck also believed in God but a God who set the whole thing going and then retired back into his heavenly abode— this is the philosophical position known as deism—so he said there is a creative life force that creates a new form that becomes a new species and the previous form disintegrates. So this life force is a transformative power.

It is necessary here to view one of the important differences between Darwin's theory of evolution and that of Lamarck.

Darwin

That a chance mutation within a species produces an animal that is better equipped for survival than the animal that has not undergone the mutation. So, over time, over generations, the genealogical line from the chance mutation survives while the previous line of animals extinguishes. There is a blind mutation and this is more favourable to the environment so it survives whereas its erstwhile cousin dies out.

Lamarck

That a change occurs in this individual through a piece of learned behaviour. This learned behaviour is then passed to the genes and so passes through to future generations. The only aspect of this theory that I want to highlight here is that Darwin's model relies for its efficacy on two blind forces: first a mutation and then an environment that favours the mutated animal rather than the un-mutated animal. Lamarck's view is that there is in the organism a principle that is able to transform the available elements to its own advantage. So Darwin's model relies on chance, leaving mutation unexplained, but Lamarck's model attributes change to the principle's capacity to transform the organism's processes and allows that these can be passed on to the gene pool and thereby to future generations. So the principle is a tranforming agent.

This is not absent in Darwin's own model because Darwin himself did incorporate Lamarck's view, but that band of disciples known as neo-Darwinians have not.

The differences between the two are as follows: that in the neo-Darwinian model (and note this was not Darwin himself who respected and incorporated Lamarck's view) everything happens without any human intentional intervention whereas Lamarck believed that free human intention did have an instrumental effect on the generational processes.

Note

1. The size of the human brain has expanded greatly since *homo erectus* two and a half million years ago. The growth of mental operations has increased with brain size. In another million years, if the brain continues to grow, then this "leap" may be understood by our descendants.

CHAPTER NINE

That which crushes the personal

Organisations, systems, ideologies crush the person if their purpose is forgotten. This is so if they are viewed as idols to be worshipped. When this happens individuals are treated as units within the system that can be sacrificed for it. The cardinal error is that the organisation is made absolute. The organisation whose role is to serve a purpose becomes instead an end in itself. The health of the organisation will be dependent upon whether that is a noble purpose or a base one and, most importantly, whether it serves that purpose which is beyond its own perimeter or makes its own structure an end in itself.

There is an inference here that the worship is being misdirected—it is being directed to the system rather than to a purpose for which it was founded. But what is this purpose? There are noble, ignoble, and impartial purposes. Let me deal first with the ignoble. A drug cartel has an ignoble purpose: it is to make money by ruining the lives of people, especially young persons. An organisation whose goal is to plant cash crops and thereby sacrifice the food supply of the local inhabitants is an ignoble purpose because the service of others is not the goal but profit. Profit is a happy consequence but an organisation whose goal is profit then does not care what it is that brings the profit. There is something though that underlies the profit. When Hitler delegated Himmler to set up an organisation known as the Final Solution to destroy all the Jews within Germany and all territories that he had conquered its purpose was ignoble. When Mao Tse-tung ordered the making of steel to export to Russia in order to curry favour and make money, sacrificing the lives of thirty million people, the organisation set up to implement this had an ignoble purpose. Any organisation whose goal is to make money irrespective of the means serves an ignoble purpose. Examples could be multiplied. Let me turn to an organisation which has a noble purpose but loses sight of its purpose and is served as an end rather than itself serving the purpose for which it was founded.

I think the term "ignoble purpose" is a faint shadow of what is really at issue here. In fact it is insulting to Jews, insulting to Chinese, insulting to those whose lives have been ruined by drug-taking, to say they are victims of an "ignoble" organisation. Such organisations are much worse than ignoble. They are evil. Melanie Klein thought that the target of envy is the creative. In one way she is right if we understand that generosity, gratitude, or forgiveness are created, but if we are speaking of someone who creates a piece of music, a painting, or a sculpture then this does not hit the mark; it is not the ultimate target of envy. There have been people who have created in this sense who have been monsters. Hitler is an example. In his early years he painted for his living. Caravaggio painted masterpieces but was a murderer. There is a far more fundamental creativity than these: it is the creation of trust, goodness, peace, and love. The organisations I have just mentioned are motivated by a violent hatred of goodness. We miss the issue if we say that these organisations are motivated by an avaricious desire for money. This is a piece of reasoning that is too rational. They are motivated by what may be called a spiritual passion. In 1938 a group of top merchant bankers at a meeting in London said that Germany would not go to war because it did not have the credits. They were closed off from passions that were more powerful than such desiccated motivations which these bankers seemed to believe were the motivating factors in human affairs. The holocaust was expensive on the German economy; Mao Tse-tung's savagery did not enhance the country's economy. No, these organisations are motivated by a hatred of goodness—yes—but it is goodness that is loathed and such organisations are determined to destroy goodness. It is this that underlies the profit motive. People who seem to be amiable and kind in their social life are sometimes merciless in business. There is a split so that there are two people resident in one body: a cruel merciless one and a courteous polite one. Underlying the profit motive is hatred of goodness.

Then there are organisations with an impartial purpose. The goal of these is neither good nor bad. What they set out to produce is not necessary for the health of the human community. For instance, firms that produce chocolate, like Cadbury, Terry's, Rowntree, or Nestlé are making something which people like and for which there is a big demand in the developed world. Yet chocolate is not absolutely necessary. Chocolate came to Europe from the New World in the sixteenth century. It was taken as a drink in Mexico among the Aztecs and known as *cacahuatl*. It was a hot bitter drink and only became sweetened, with sugar from Cuba, by the Spanish descendents of Hernán Cortés. So until the sixteenth century it was not known in Europe. It only began to be produced as a solid which people could buy and eat as a snack just over a hundred years ago. It is a foodstuff that people can do without. It is not essential yet numerous people like it. A firm producing it is not serving a noble purpose but it is not an ignoble purpose either. It serves an impartial purpose. The firms that make chocolate make a profit. If the profit motive smothers the impartial purpose then the organisation becomes corrupted. The chocolate produced in the Ivory Coast of west Africa on farms where the chocolate beans are grown were planted there in the 1980s as a cash crop under the inspiration of the dictator Félix Houphouet-Boigny. Today these cocoa beans on the farms in the Ivory Coast are being harvested by child slaves and this is known to the large chocolate firms mentioned above but, because the profit motive has become the dominant purpose, so these firms have done nothing to prevent the use of child slavery. They have turned a blind eye to what is going on. There is also a history of exploitation of labour in the chocolate making industry. In the early years of the nineteenth century cocoa beans were harvested on the two islands of São Tomé and Principe, under Portuguese governance, with "indentured labour". These were blacks brought from Angola and forced in chain gangs to harvest these beans. This was known by Cadbury but they pretended ignorance until the journalist Henry Nevinson revealed it (Off, 2008).

I have given here just one example of an impartial industry which has become ignoble because the profit motive has smothered its prime purpose which is to provide the taste buds of those in the developed world with a sweet delight. This is symptomatic of a social system in which countries with an acquired taste for a particular foodstuff exploit poorer countries that are able to provide these products at a cheaper price than they can. For instance, in the course of the nineteenth century, huge areas of Australia were shorn of their native fauna and dedicated instead to the production of cattle and sheep to feed Britain, the home country, with the beef and lamb to which they were accustomed. A social system built up of numerous interlocking smaller enterprises are part of the world in which we live, eat, and have our being. Like the air we breathe we are not conscious of them. These social systems enter the very interstices of our being. They enter the inner sanctum of the personality. The system is outside and inside the personality. As already mentioned (see Chapter Six), Talcott Parsons has expanded Freud's concept of the superego to include these cultural imperatives that exist inside the individual.

I have taken food as an example because nothing distinguishes cultures more than their different eating habits. These are learned as soon as a baby is weaned. It is necessary here to give consideration to the kind of learning which is involved. How does an Indian baby learn to like curry, a Chinese baby learn to like bamboo shoots, a French baby learn to like snails, or an English baby learn to like egg and bacon?

The word "learning" does not seem quite right. There is a sense in which these habits are acquired through osmosis and yet there is a learning of which we are not conscious. A man whose sight was poor had a corneal transplant done which improved the sight in his left eye but initially, although the retina in the left eye was functioning better than before the operation, he saw less well. Then after two weeks his brain re-calibrated, as he put it, and then he saw better. This is how he describes it:

> Seeing, which takes place in the brain, not the eye, is the result of the retinal input to the brain, and of learning—mostly unconscious. For twenty years my brain had repeatedly had to re-learn how to deliver the best "seeing" from diminished retinal input and it had done this impressively well. This time there was an increase of retinal input and, until my brain had done some re-learning, this was confusing so that although what I saw was excitingly different and qualitatively better, for a time, in some ways, I saw worse. (Mann, 2008, p. 162)

We need to invoke here the level of operation that has become familiar through the investigations of neuroscientists. For instance, subjects who were given stimulus cards did not know that they had seen something that stimulated them erotically but then a PET scan revealed that more blood rushed to a particular part of the brain. Therefore something was happening which was not consciously known. There was a time lag between the brain registration and the conscious knowing.

In Chapter One I observed that there was in the individual both the created and uncreated and that what differentiated these two was that the elements inside the personality were either the products of the *creative principle* or were untouched by it. The social system enters the personality unbidden. It enters through a pressure. This pressure finds its purchase through the individual's fear of loneliness. There is a strong desire in everyone to belong, to be part of the collective and not to be estranged by the group. Colin Turnbull in his study of the pygmies (1961) describes how a few hours of isolation was a terrible punishment for a tribal member. So there are two ways in which something enters into the personality: either through pressure driven by the fear of isolation or through an inner creative act.

Freud cried out loud that neurosis was the consequence of repressing sexual desire, the kind of sexual desire that was condemned by society, the society of his day. Repressing meant, in Freud's own definition, removing attention from something. He wrote: "… the mechanisms of repression have at least this one thing in common: a withdrawal of the cathexis of energy …" (1915d, pp. 154–155). The word *cathexis* is a translation of the German word *Besetzung* which means that a certain amount of psychical energy is attached to an idea, a group of ideas, a part of the body or to an object (Laplanche & Pontalis, 1973). But when we think of energy we need to incorporate it into a personal act. This is a different foundation though from that of Freud. The source of action for Freud was in instincts which are governed by the thrust for survival. When the survival need is satisfied then a state of equilibrium is re-established. The ego here is governed by the instincts under this principle. In Freud's schema the ego, as it were, sits on the surface of an instinctual sea like a cork on the water. What is here being claimed is that the "governor" is the ego which is a creative force whose source is from within the living organism and, although it looks almost nothing yet this "cork on the water" is the source that holds together the living organism. This has been succinctly expressed by Maurice Blondel as already mentioned (see Chapter Three, page seven). The *"little as nothing"* that Blondel (1893) speaks of is what unifies, and this is the subjective: "The subjective is precisely that which cannot be known either in function of mathematics or in function of sensible observation, because it is that which constitutes their bond and introduces unity amid the multiplicity" (1984, pp. 103–104). It is a case where emphasis changes what is seen like reverse perspective. It is that Freud places the emphasis on the instincts upon which rests the ego, like a cork on the water, whereas Blondel takes this *"little as nothing"* as the organising principle of the human being.

We discharge energy when we are angry, when we hate; we conserve energy when we love. The anger is I believe because the ego, instead of being the principle of synthesis, has become the slave to the stimuli bombarding it from within and from without.

Attention is I think the kind of psychic activity that Freud had in mind when he said that a withdrawal of *Besetzung* is what constituted repression. In other words a withdrawal of *attention* is what we mean by repression. In *attention* there is a concentration of psychic energy. So one needs to consider what it means to *attend* to something. What is the difference between something which is *attended* to and something which is not *attended* to? It is clear that the *attending to* has an effect upon that which is the object of *attention*. If this were not so then there would be no difference between something which is repressed and something which is not repressed. *Attention*, as an act, has an effect upon the object; it is changed by the *attention*. Wilfred Bion clearly understood this because on the horizontal axis of the grid he starts, after column two, with notation and then moves to *attention* and then on to enquiry. Bion (1963) associates *attention* with reverie. Now, reverie is a state in which the mind *attends* to something but not in a way which excludes the rest of what is real. If I focus in a determined way upon something, someone, or part of someone, I do so from the outer part of my personality and draw thereby the inner being towards it. The inner is dragged into servitude of those senses which are focused upon the object. The whole personality then is enslaved to the outer object. Reverie is an activity whose source is in the central being of the personality. The being of the person is characterised by its attribute of *in-relation*. Reverie is a bringing of the object into the realm of the inner being. Freud did not use the word *reverie* but his recommendations to psychoanalysts imply it: "The rule for the doctor may be expressed: 'He should withhold all conscious influences from his capacity to attend, and give himself over completely to his 'unconscious memory'" (1912e, p. 112). He makes it clear that his resource must be from his own personal experiences:

> ... the sacrifice involved in laying oneself open to another person without being driven to it by illness is amply rewarded. Not only is one's aim of learning to know what is hidden in one's own mind far more rapidly attained and with less expense of affect, but impressions and convictions will be gained in relation to oneself which will be sought in vain from studying books and attending lectures. (1912e, pp. 116–117)

He explains that these experiences within oneself are the source for understanding the patient and these are personal impressions and convictions. The healing factor is one person coming into relation with another. And, as has been referred to, the inner being of the person is *in-relation*. What is healing, therefore, is the inner being of one coming into relation with the inner being of another. The creative seed is in the inner being and this fertilises the inner being of the other. There is no intermediary between them. Time and place are not capable of interfering with this fertilising relationship.

This idea where Freud says that the doctor should withhold all conscious influences is the same as Bion's *reverie* and also of Marion Milner's distinction between attention with a narrow focus and attention with a wide focus. She puts it clearly: "I myself had learnt when writing the Joanna Field books, for instance, about having observed that there were two kinds of attention, both necessary, a wide unfocused stare, and a narrow focused penetrating kind, and that the wide kind brought remarkable changes in perception and enrichment of feeling" (1987, p. 81).

Basically if someone is focused upon his own pains, what is required is that he opens himself to the immensity of being. This cannot be done by a focus upon the inner bitterness and the cause of it, but rather what is needed is an expansion of his personality. I have just used a soft and easy phrase, "expansion of the personality" but how on earth does that happen? Charles Dickens has a go at expressing this in that lovely fable of his, *A Christmas Carol*. In this story Ebenezer Scrooge, who is a sour, mean, bitter old man, is visited on Christmas Eve night by three ghosts: the Ghost of Christmas Past, the Ghost of Christmas Present and the Ghost of Christmas Yet to Come. What do these ghosts represent? Scrooge is old; his erstwhile partner, Jacob Marley, seven years dead, as Dickens puts it, comes to him. For some reason death became a reality for Scrooge. He had always known that he would die but it was a truth that was outside himself. Suddenly on that Christmas Eve his death, which is now not far away, came to him as real. He had seen a coffin passing on a waggon as he was travelling home that same day, and then as he reaches his house the door knocker becomes Jacob Marley in an hallucinatory moment. What we cannot know is quite why this happens to him. He tries to pass it off by saying that the ghosts that he sees are only the product of undigested cheese.

Then there is the case of Siddhartha. He lived in his father's palace and there enjoyed an idyllic paradise. He knew nothing of illness, of old age, or of death until Channa, his charioteer, took him out of the palace on a ride through the countryside and there Siddhartha saw a man who was ill with a disease, then he saw an old man, and then the body of a man who was dead. This shook the young man out of a trance into the knowledge of the world, so that night he left his father's palace and went into the deer park and donned the poor robes of an ascetic, and was there for seven years before he achieved Enlightenment and became the Buddha, the awakened one. What happened to Siddhartha is told here in the form of a fable. What then is the state of mind of which the palace is a symbol? It seems that young Siddhartha was in an hypnotised state. He had a young wife, we are told, and also a child, and one is led to understand that he was in a privileged position—shut off from all disquiet and discomfort; that life was a sort of dream. My sense is that young Siddhartha knew that disease, old age, and death existed but that they were not real for him. I know that the Statue of Liberty exists but I have not seen it; then one day I sail into New York harbour in a ship and see the statue with my own eyes. I step off the boat and go up to the statue and feel it with my hands. It does not become real until my senses have become engaged with it. Similarly I hear that my father has died but it is not until I see his dead body and then see the coffin lowered into the grave that I begin to know it. There has to be some inner revolution for me to know it.

There is a difference between intellectual knowledge, sensual knowledge, and emotional knowing. To illustrate this I want first to mention a personal story. My mother died in late September one year. I knew she had died, I went to the funeral. I had seen the coffin lowered into the grave, I had thrown earth onto the coffin. So I knew it as a fact and I will call this factual knowledge *pragmatic knowledge*, but I did not know it emotionally. Then five years later I had this dream: my mother was coming towards me and she looked incredibly real. Sometimes in dreams a figure or place has a real-ness about it that seems to mean something. Then a voice came from the side and said: "Is it real or is it a dream?", and I answered: "It's a dream because my mother is in it." When I woke I knew now that my mother was dead, that she was no more. I was sad and cried. For me to know emotionally that my mother was dead had taken five years. So what does "emotionally" mean: this word that we toss off with such gay abandon? What was the difference between my knowing that my mother was dead when I went to her funeral and when I woke up after that dream? The point of the dream is that she looked very real but I knew that I was seeing her through a dream lens and not through … the way she looked was not what told me whether what I saw was the truth but rather it was necessary for me to know the medium through which I saw it. In this experience I knew the medium. It was an experience of knowing the medium. Or look at it differently: the pragmatic me that had been to the funeral was now able to assert itself against the dream in which she was alive. Usually when we are in a dream we believe it but here there was a knowledge that it was a dream. There were two voices in this dream. One was asking, "Is it real or is it a dream?" This voice is wanting to know which of these two states was operating here. So there is a me who does not know and then there is a pragmatic me who says, "It's a dream because my mother is in it." I consider there is another way of thinking about this. In the dream she appeared very real. I think it means that the realness was because she was outside me. When I recalled earlier that at the funeral I did not know emotionally that she was dead, so if she was still alive, where was she?

To know something emotionally requires a double engagement. The inner me has to be fastened to the outer event. The two have to bond together. The outer event has to be created by the inner. The neuroscientist, Antonio Damasio, has made a valuable distinction between *core consciousness* and *extended consciousness*. What I have referred to above as *pragmatic knowledge* is what would be included by Damasio within *extended consciousness*. It was the *pragmatist* who said "It's a dream because my mother is in it", but the *pragmatist* was saying it within the dream. The dream comes from the core of me, from the inner me. I now know it in my core. I know it because I have created what I know. The *core* is a creator. The extended part of the personality is the *pragmatist*. It is that part of the personality which records outer events. This *pragmatist* which relates to the outer world of sensations is what Freud called the *ego*.

I will elaborate this further and in order to do this I need first to relate something else that someone told me. This man's mother died when he was two years old but it did not seem to be something that he felt. It was a fact like Russia is a large country, dogs' bodies are covered with fur, water converts to steam when heated to 100°C. Two things were very strong in him: he adored his father and he had great insight and feeling for anyone, especially a child, who was sad or grieving. His mother's essence had been thrust into his father whom he loved passsionately, and he had ingested his mother's maternal function into himself so she had not died. What I mean here is that insight into himself and his processes were very developed. He had taken inner possession of what Winnicott called *primary maternal preoccupation*.

What I am saying here is that the functions of the person who has died are still living so they have not died. Well, the obvious question then is—did this man lose his love for his father and his caring for people, especially children, who were sad or depressed? I think the answer requires close attention. I will revert now to my own expereince. The taking in of the maternal function was there already in me before my mother died. I had probably taken it in within the first two years of life. But I had not just taken in my mother's function but that of others also. I have taken in the spirit of the mind of great thinkers whom I have studied. The individual teachings are manifestations of the man's mental outlook. This has been so for me of Freud, of Jung, of Socrates, of Plato, of Thomas Aquinas, of G. K. Chesterton, of Isaiah Berlin, of Vladimir Solovyov, of John Macmurray, of Meister Eckhart, of Tolstoy, and of Wilfred Bion. I had taken in my mother's mode of taking in "the other"; it is an early learning by osmosis. When my mother truly died emotionally, in that dream in which I saw her outside coming towards me, I no longer took in the whole of Freud, of Jung, etc. but I was now myself and took in not the whole thinker indiscriminately but according to a Neville lens. In other words I took in reality as a whole but through the particular lens called "Neville". I no longer made a fragment into the whole but the whole into the whole. I remember something that used to annoy me about my mother. She could not see a fault in someone she loved and admired. She would turn even the most glaring vices into virtues. She was able to persuade herself of the goodness of something which seemed to me so obviously bad. She was also not able to take criticism; I think this means that the origin behind her seeing her admired figures as faultless was her own faultlessness. So she saw the people she loved through this lens of hers. I also as a baby drank in this mode of hers. To this day I tend to do this with those admired figures that I have mentioned above and yet, today, I manage not to. The way in which my mother's mode had become ingested into me was almost elemental in me. I was also persuaded to her viewpoint even in such basic matters as taste. For instance, my mother used to praise the virtues of a Spanish brandy and I would drink it believing it to be the elixir of the gods, but one day I drank it and awoke out of this maternal hypnosis. "My God this is foul, this brandy." Everything Spanish was good in my mother's eyes—its brandy, its wine, bullfights, flamenco dancing, Franco, and even the Spanish Inquisition. I think that when, five years after my mother's death, I knew that this was a dream, the maternal mode of taking things in was now outside myself. My own me-ness was now living. Before that, when someone was reverenced, then all of him was good whether it be Freud, Shakespeare, Wilfred Bion, Tolstoy, Mozart, Darwin, the Buddha, or Jesus. Great though these people were—and I do not wish to equate them—yet each one of them, yes even Buddha and Jesus, were at times wrong, in error. I believe that when I had that dream this maternal mode of taking in was now outside me and I could take in critically, and this critical way of taking in seemed really to be me. But there was established a love for my mother despite this slice of self-centredness within her. This was now real love and not a love based on a projection of my own selfhood.

I think the matter goes further than that though. I think that when I had that dream it coincided with the capacity to separate the good that came from my mother from the bad. What is the difference between good and bad? I am saying here that my mother's conviction that all things Spanish were good was a piece of bad functioning in her—but why? What is wrong with it? It remind me of a statement from Chesterton: "Truth, of course, must of necessity be stranger than fiction, for we have made fiction to suit ourselves" (1905, p. 60). I am suggesting here that this love of all things Spanish was somehow to suit herself. Meister Eckhart points out that making oneself into a receptacle for God's grace is in itself a self-enhancement (1981, p. 200). Making Spain into the good comes about because somehow my mother is making a fragment of the world into the good *to the exclusion of all else*. And I knew that this was true because in making all things Spanish good she was silently disparaging all things Portuguese. This is the difference between good and bad. In the good no thing is excluded and it is the infinite which is good whereas the bad is a perversion of this. It is when a fragment is made into a whole that other elements of reality are then excluded.

There is knowledge that there is a coming together of an outer event and an inner receptivity to that event. In the receptivity there is a going-out towards. A search is in progress. There is some dim knowledge that the life being lived is lacking something, something crucial. Then there is a coming together of the inner and the outer which seems miraculous.

This was the huge mutation that occurred at the dawn of civilisation. When humans started to paint in the caves of Altamira, Lascaux, and Chauvet in Europe and in the Pilbarra region of Australia it was a sign that this inner being had become released from the stranglehold of the senses. Clearly those ancestors of ours living in those caves twenty to thirty thousand years ago *attended* to those bison and other animals which they painted upon the ceilings of their caves. One effect of *attention* is to bring what belongs to the realm of the senses from the outer sense-dominated sphere of the personality into the inner. It is that the inner being draws the sense object into its realm so that it gives a particularity to the inner realm. The inner realm is in relation. This is what differentiates sanity from madness. When the inner being is enslaved, annihilated in fact, by the stimuli bombarding the organism through the senses then the individual is mad, but when the inner being holds itself *in-relation* to the outer world through the intellectual faculty that grasps being then there is a sane mind within the organism. So the question is why did those cavemen draw the particular into the relational realm of being? There are two questions that need to be addressed here: first is the relational nature of being and the second is the evolution of the brain. Here I will reflect for a moment on the relational nature of being.

The planets are in relation to the sun; the sun is in relation to the other stars of the galaxy. This galaxy, the Milky Way, is in relation to the other galaxies swirling around through space. Within the atom the electron is related to the proton. It is inherent in the nature of reality that it is *in-relation*. I believe that this is why Christian theologians declared that there is an *in-relation* mode within the godhead, known as the Trinity.

In psychoanalytic literature we hear a lot about undifferentiation between self and object or a merged state of affairs between self and object. This is the point at which we need to examine more closely those uncreated elements in the personality and where they come from and how they enter the individual. There are two modes in which someone links to another—either by external attachment or by interior communion. Thomas Ogden has written in a recent article: "… we gain access to the unconscious dimension of experience by looking *into* conscious experience, not by looking 'behind' it or 'beneath' it" (2009, p. 149). The latter is undefined except by its existence. I think this is what Ogden means here. There is no restricting factor. A flower is not an animal but the only thing which existence is not is non-existence. If I sink my surface, sensation based individuality into my existence I am in brotherhood with the stars, the minerals, the plants, the animals, human beings, and all historical events.

The view that the human person is subject to the infinite rather than the finite allows for plasticity whereas the latter attachment solidifies what needs to be flexible. This sense of being in brotherhood or sisterhood with the universe was beautifully expressed by St. Francis of Assisi in his famous *Canticle of the Sun*:

> Praise to Thee, my Lord, for Sister Moon and the stars
> Which thou has set in the heavens,
> Clear, precious, and fair.
>
> Praise to Thee, my Lord, for Brother Wind,
> For air and cloud, for calm and all weather,
> By which Thou supportest life I call Thy creatures.
>
> Praise to Thee, my Lord, for Sister Water,
> Who is so useful and humble,
> Precious and pure.
>
> Praise to Thee, my Lord, for Brother Fire,
> By whom Thou lightest the night;
> He is lovely and pleasant, mighty and strong.
> (Shirley-Price, 1959)

There is a relation between things in the whole vastness of the universe. There is that beautiful plea when a physician approached Francis with a hot fiery implement to cauterise his eye he said, "Treat me gently Brother Fire."

There is a philosophical belief originating with John Locke that all knowledge comes through the senses and that the mind is a *tabula rasa*, a wax tablet that takes the impressions forced upon it. In this model the *creative principle* has no theoretical place. I emphasise the word "theoretical" because, although not articulated, it is implied. Hence even the most devoted disciple of Locke cannot avoid knowing that there is a selection of stimuli, but the principle within, by which that selection is made, is ignored. Freud was in this same tradition. So, for instance, he speaks of *sublimation* whereby an instinctual impulse is made socially useful but ignores the principle through which this occurs. He does not say how it happens but his mode of expression implies that he thinks that it is forced somehow upon the mind. The ego is that part of the personality that faces the external world; it is the umbrella word for the senses. Yet no philosopher or thinker of any depth can be satisfied with that, so Freud says that this ego is deepened through identifications. In other words it has a quality that transcends the wax tablet.

It is not enough, however, to say that the mind is a wax tablet and that stimuli are forced upon it. What we arrive at is that the mind can exist in two states: one is the wax tablet state and the other is the *creative principle* state. But the wax tablet state is not one that is just passive but rather the stimuli, whatever they may be, become endowed with all the force of a command. What we have to ask then is what is it in the personality that so endows it?

CHAPTER TEN

All-inclusive principle

In the Introduction I mentioned that if the process existing between the two poles was infused with a certain quality then these two poles become persons. In this chapter I want to examine this quality.

A woman who had many signs that her mother did not love her one day said: "You know it would have been much better for me if my mother had told me that she had not wanted me. I could have dealt with that."

If her mother had told her that she had not wanted her she would have trusted her because it was contained in her mother's mind, so that mother would have been living it rather than being lived by it which was her daughter's experience. She was a latchkey child and once just before Christmas her mother told her she would give her some lovely presents on Christmas Day but she went out on Christmas Eve, got drunk and the next morning there were no presents for her daughter. In fact what was needed was for her mother to tell herself, in other words to create into her own possession that she had not wanted this child. If she had done this then her daughter's experience would have been different. She would not have needed either to have told her daughter that she was not wanted.

This principle was enunciated by George Eliot in her novel *Middlemarch*. The love of Lydgate for Rosamund is a sub-plot of the novel. Rosamund is a *femme fatale* and after a time Lydgate realises that she does not love him, but far worse, says George Eliot, is: "… the certainty 'She will never love me much', is easier to bear than the fear 'I shall love her no more'" (1973, p. 702). The overarching principle here is that it drives not only her, this patient of mine, mad but that anyone goes into madness if they are not able to love. This answer to my questioning came through an understanding of this woman's problem, yet my state of enquiry related not just to this woman sitting in front of me but to something general that applied to her, to me, and to people across cultures and back through history for at least eleven millennia or since the dawning of civilization. It must also have been that when I realised this, when my heart was grasped by this statement, I was receptive to it, but in a way in which I had not been before. My own mind was in a state of enquiry, searching out for it. So the principle that madness arises if someone is not able to love has sufficient abstraction within it to apply to a description of humanity in all its many forms. When I say that it has *sufficient abstraction* this does not mean that it is just a Platonic idea but rather that it is a reality—but a reality that suffuses sensual reality with its all-inclusive possibility. It is a reality in the human forum like volume, density, or gravity in nature that permeates the sensation dominated world. Such a reality is capable of being a common denominator that entirely respects the individuality and freedom of each person, and as a principle is capable of being used to solve each individual patient's problem and does not force any individual into a framework which does not fit. So, for instance, to say that a clay brick is of a specified volume detracts nothing from its individual quality; so also if one specifies its density, its particular shape and colour are not diminished. With regard to human beings there is a different set of principles that govern the individual qualities. In physical bodies there is gravity that has within each body a magnetic attraction, that makes one body be in relation to another. Between human beings there is a human-level equivalent of gravity. What is this? Gravity can give us a clue: that there is some linkage between me and another but that this is not just at the gravity level but at the specifically human level. Whereas gravity is an inherent constituent of either a stone or a planet, within a human being this relational element is something that is in existence but to become humanly real it is not just there like gravity is there: to be present it has to be desired.

There is a further principle that is closely linked to this. It is that as soon as someone starts to love she experiences mental pain. It may be sadness, it may be guilt, it may be regret, it may be disappointment, or it may be shame. Hatred expels the pain whereas love embraces it. Therefore one reason why love is avoided is because it opens the person to pain. Madness is an anaesthetic against pain. These then are inter-related principles. One of the defining principles of sanity is the capacity to love and madness is the inability to love. It is no good an analyst pointing out to a patient that he denies pain, denies guilt, denies disappointment. The task is to expand the individual's capacity to love and this will bring with it a knowledge of guilt, of pain, and of disappointment.

There is another ancillary principle that is implied in the statement that my patient made about her mother. It was clear that something prevented her mother from embracing the truth that she had not wanted this child of hers. It may have been that this is not a feeling that a mother is supposed to have, and here is another ancillary principle: that under constraint a truth cannot be embraced. For it to be capable of being embraced someone needs to be entirely free of constraint. And then a further principle arises from this.

It is that had her mother been able to embrace it and thus to say it to her child, or more important been able to say it to herself, her hatred would have been contained within her own psyche and not discharged; then her child's experience would have been quite different. Instead of experiencing neglectful or hateful activities of the mother, she would have known a distress of her mother's. Mother's distress would not have been expressed in neglectful acts towards her daughter but transformed into inner knowledge. So the principle here is that the encompassing of a truth within the psyche generates understanding towards the other. So my patient's experience as a child would have been different.

There is another ancillary principle that flows from this. It is that I see the world through the lens of my own psychological structure. If that structure is based on hate and discharge, the way I see the world is quite different from the way I see the world if I have embraced what is within me. These then are the abstract principles which I am able to use as instruments to solve the problem that my patient brings me. As they apply to me as much as to my patient they give me a platform from which to judge the state of self-awareness. Knowing myself, to the extent to which I am able to achieve it, is the fundamental yardstick through which I am able to understand the problems of my patients.

This principle which I have called love requires a different name. The use of the word love suggests that it is a something which I possess, which is a misunderstanding. To return to the analogy of gravity, planet Earth does not possess gravity; it is a principle inherent in the planet which unites it with the sun and other planets in the solar system and in turn unites the solar system to the rest of the galaxy and the galaxy to the whole of the universe. There is then a uniting principle both within the psyche of each individual and between individuals. This uniting principle is knowledge linked to love. Knowing and loving are linked entities. It is that loving or liking is based on some element of similarity. Meister Eckhart wrote: "All attraction and desire and love come from that which is like, because all things are attracted by and love what is like them" (1981, p. 214). Eckhart has taken this from Aristotle's *Ethics*: "There is a saying, 'Like, and be like', and the best proof of its truth is found in the friendship of good men" (Book 8, Ch. 5). The loving is a desire, an emotion that drives the knowing, whereas the knowing itself comes about through being in it. It is a form of being which is knowledge. The word "intuition" does not carry the love in it. We need to find a word or phrase that includes them both. I suggest *wisdom-of-heart*. Wisdom conveys something that is an endowment from above. The wise man has allowed himself to be possessed of wisdom. He has given his heart to something that is outside himself and yet includes him. Wisdom is transcendent and yet immanent and so it is of the heart and not of the surface of the personality. It is this *wisdom-of-heart* that is the principle that creates two individuals into people who are in relation to one another.

If the analyst's or psychotherapist's psychological place is in the sphere of this principle then from this viewpoint, which is either deeper or higher than psychological models proper, all of them can be encompassed. At the moment within psycho-analytic discourse the models are restricted within a narrow field. We are all familiar with Freud's theory of repression, with Jung's typology, with Kohut's theory of mirroring, with Melanie Klein's theory of the paranoid-schizoid and depressive positions, with Bion's theory of container-contained, but these are just those models contained within the official psychoanalytic textbooks: there are many other models which are often apt. For instance, the classical learning theory is often applicable, as are Piaget's theory of object constancy, Stefan Zweig's theory of intensified passion in the handicapped individual, Blondel's theory that emotional action takes its colouring from the object towards which it tends, Macmurray's theory that the self is an agent that produces thought, Tolstoy's theory that suicide is the outcome of extreme narcissism, Hermann Hesse's view that suicide is a state of mind rather than a particular act, the Buddha's theory of *dukka*, and the historian Arthur Bryant's view that stifled creativity leads to destructiveness. Chesterton's view is that it is through faith that we know the existence of other people. Kierkegaard's view is that it is the act of choice that endows the individual with nobility. This deeper principle, *wisdom-of-heart*, that I have tried to enunciate, enables the clinician to encompass all these and many other different models. *Wisdom-of-heart* is not something learned as a process of reasoning following the processing of sensations. It is acquired through being in relation to wisdom as manifest in a person, and being startled by a new unfamiliarity which changes the heart. It is not an abstract idea but a reality whose core is emotional and personal. The difference between wisdom and conclusions reached from reasoning is that the source of the former comes from the principle of oneness that permeates all reality in the way that volume or density are within all the variety, whereas ... the latter finds a link between things based upon a "sensual similarity".

I have referred in the Introduction to the way in which a mother, who is able to reflect on her own experience, even when that has not been satisfactory, endows her baby thereby with the capacity to relate. What I refer to as *wisdom-of-heart* is exemplified in such an instance. The mother who has "mental space to relate to her own relations with others" has *wisdom-of-heart* but how has she acquired it? One could say that this mother that Hobson refers to has received this capacity from her mother and she from her mother and so on but this does not tell us how this benign genealogy came about. It also assumes that the way this has happened has been from mother to child but can someone ever achieve this *wisdom-of-heart* from a source other than the mother? And is the generative quality the ability to *think about* past experiences?

Thinking about is the surface manifestation of a deeper process. What I want to do is to try to name that. There are basic assumptions that govern the way we see things. Now, it is assumed in the Freudian world that the assumptions on which this philosophy is built are the right ones. Yet I believe this is a serious error. There were some basic assumptions in Freud's thinking which were wrong, badly wrong. He rejected religion.

Religion like science is full of errors but it has some pearls of wisdom which have been enunciated by the mystics. So I will take some basic assumptions as Freud expresses them in *Civilization and its Discontents*. His first assumption is that what human beings most want and what they strive for is happiness:

> We … turn to the … question of what men themselves show by their behaviour to be the purpose and intention of their lives. What do they demand of life and wish to achieve in it? The answer to this can hardly be in doubt. They strive after happiness; they want to become happy and to remain so. The endeavour has two sides, a positive and negative aim. It aims, on the one hand, at an absence of pain and unpleasure, and, on the other, at the experiencing of strong feelings of pleasure. (1930a, p. 76)

Yet this has been opposed strongly by thinkers down the ages; for instance, the philosopher, John Macmurray says:

> Freedom is, I am assured, the pearl of great price for which, if we are wise, we shall be prepared to sell all our possessions, to buy it. The ancient and widespread belief that the supreme good of human life is happiness—for all its persuasiveness—is false. Freedom has a higher value than happiness; and this is what we recognize when we honour those who have been ready to sacrifice happiness, and even life itself, for freedom's sake. (1949, p. 2)

So we have here two opposed positions. They cannot both be right but let us notice that both are asserted with absolute certitude. So which is right? We have just quoted Freud as saying, "It aims, on the one hand, at an absence of pain and unpleasure, and, on the other, at the experiencing of strong feelings of pleasure."

Yet is there any possibility of living life with no pain? Is this not some fool's paradise that is being recommended? If someone really followed this, and people do try to follow such a prescription without Freud guiding them to do so, he would be constantly running from every situation that was painful. In my relationships with others there are always difficulties that challenge me to do things which are painful. I can steer my life in such a way that I avoid them. Is that not precisely the position of the neurotic? That he evades what is uncomfortable, what is uncongenial so does not truly live? Does it not force itself upon us that what we have to do if we are to live a full life is to accept pain as well as joy? In fact if we avoid pain we avoid joy also. The key word here is "accept". If we follow Freud's belief that his symbolic individual is one who aims at an absence of pain and an experiencing of pleasure then avoiding an aspect of life, of living, is his governing belief. The difference here is between "avoiding" and "accepting". Consider Marion Milner's life's aim:

> What I want is, not when I came to die to say, "I've been as useful as I know how"—I ought to want that but I don't. I want to feel that I have "lived". But what on earth do I mean by that? I mean something silly and Sunday paperish like "plumbing the depths of human experience", or "drinking life to the dregs". What nonsense it sounds. I suppose I've got a Sunday paper mind. I don't want to be of service to a good cause, so it's no good pretending that I do. Maybe it's colossal egotism, but I want a share in everything in the world, the bad as well as the good. The world is so marvellous, I want to grasp it, to partake of it, to embrace it, to feel every part of me vibrating with it. (1934, p. 23)

She wants a share in the good as well as the bad, the painful as well as the pleasurable.

Do we need to go so far as Macmurray and say that freedom is what people want most dearly and not happiness? Let us look at it more closely. In what does freedom consist? I am a free man if I accept, accept deeply, that which is. I cannot help quoting that fourteenth century English mystic who wrote in *The Epistle of Privy Counsel* the following: "… therefore come down into the lowest point of thy wit, the which some man holdest by very proof that it is the highest, and think on the simplest manner, but by some man the wisest, not what thyself is, but that thyself is" (McCann, 1952, emphasis added).

Yet this is Freud's own view. His description of a neurotic symptom is that the inner impulse has not been accepted and therefore resulted in a substitute condition and it is the non-acceptance that leads to the formation of a neurotic symptom. What Macmurray introduces is "value". There is a value, he believes, in acceptance. For Freud there is a value in avoidance, or is it that he believes that the instinct to avoid pain and seek pleasure is something that human beings are driven by as if they were machines? The question here is, does "acceptance" of this fact change the fact? It seems that Freud has accepted the fact that we are instinctually driven to avoid pain and seek pleasure but he has done more than this. He has said that this is the only goal of action available to human beings. It is that other sources of action are banished. "Value" is something chosen; it is not something that *has* to be done. Freud's position is that human beings have no choice: they *have to* avoid pain and seek pleasure. Value, though, implies that there is something in the human being that has a command over the stimuli that bombard it from within and from without. That, having accepted the fact that we are driven to avoid pain and seek pleasure, opens the personality to other possibilities. Acceptance does not mean a fatalistic surrender. It means that the human being recognises what is.

There are two theories here: one is that human beings, and life itself in any of its forms, is no different from an inanimate lump of matter, and so moved by elements outside itself; and the contrary view, that humans and all living things have a source of initiation entirely from within the organism. Freud's metapsychological theory is therefore determinist but his clinical theory contradicts this. *The Interpretation of Dreams* tells of impulses, wishes, which have not been acknowledged and therefore, central to his way of thinking, is that there is within the personality a faculty that acknowledges or does not acknowledge or, to use the language I have been using, accept or not accept. But the problem is that this is pasted onto a background that says no such choice is available to the personality. This obscures the central significance of acceptance. Acceptance is a faculty in the personality that transcends the inner and outer stimuli. It transcends it and is immanent. It is a quality like volume that permeates the material entity and yet is not it so transcends it. Freud's theory as elaborated in *The Interpretation of Dreams* is that here in the dream life is the beginning of an acceptance of wishes and impulses. The act of acceptance anoints the personality with freedom. If the stimulus, wish, or impulse is not accepted then the individual is captive to it. Acceptance is an act that frees. From where in the personality does acceptance proceed?

I have until now used the word "accept" but it is not adequate. It too easily bears the tone of reluctant resignation. What is meant by acceptance is a creation of what is. This means that there is an inner spirit that wills what is. There are two alternatives to that which is: either the *is-ness* is hated or loved. Love is creation. That which exists needs to be created. It can either be created or uncreated. Let me quote from a friend of mine who is a painter. He had spent forty years of his adult life in a passionate enquiry into the nature of light and how to transform that through the medium of pigment onto the canvas, and then at the age of sixty-eight he was struck blind. He was entirely blind without a hint of sight. When this happened to him I wrote him a letter of sympathy about a year later. This came to me in his letter of reply:

> My exhibition went incredibly well and I sold all but two of the oils and several gouaches. It was certainly partly as a result of all the publicity I got. I was on *Midweek* on Radio 4 with Libby Purves and the gallery had twelve enquiries in the first hour and a half after the programme. I suppose it is pretty surprising that I am able to go on painting now that I am totally blind but now that I have been doing it for a year and a half, I take it for granted. What is really wonderful for me is how good my painting chums, and the buying public, bless them, think that these new, blind paintings are. People have actually said that they think that this was my best show to date, how can that be? Since finishing the Cadaques subjects I have been painting Frances sitting in one of two chairs in my studio, a large armchair and one of those ubiquitous plastic garden chairs which I have put on a table so that I am looking across at Frances rather than down on her. I position myself very close so that I can understand how she is sitting by touch but I have also devised a system of measuring using my white sticks so as to work out what she would look like from where I am. I then mark positions on my canvas with little blobs of Blutac—at present about sixty on a painting—so that I know where I am by feel. One of the great innovations is that since I have no perception of light or colour, I can make things any colour I like. These paintings have a simple but much more highly coloured design so that in one I might make the chair bright red and then in the next, I make it green. Likewise the background can be any colour I choose. I paint Frances a natural colour and only paint her clothes colours that she wears, mostly black therefore. Again, the funny thing is that chaps seems to think that these paintings are very good and the living painter I most revere, Leon Kossoff, was so complimentary that I almost wept. So as you can see, Neville, things are going fine and there is definitely life after blindness and a jolly good life at that.

This friend of mine had accepted what had happened. He views himself and sees that he is now blind; it is a scientific fact. He then turns and makes use of what is available to him. If you think of the body as a workman's set of tools he sees what is available to him and uses what is there. He cannot use his eyes any more so he now uses his sense of touch, his hands, with a stick to measure, and so on. I quote this because it is such a remarkable example of acceptance. It is easy to imagine a parallel case where a painter went blind and became bitter. The act of acceptance is a creation. But where does this come from?

Somehow, in a way which is mysterious, particularly mysterious to the modern scientific mind, there is a source of action from within the living organism. Some neuroscientists come close to this when they say that an action finds its source in the brain but is the brain the initiator? These scientists place the brain at the service of the thrust for survival. The thrust for survival is what patterns and drives the brain. There is no room here for acceptance; there is no room for the representation of what is. Acceptance, representation of what is, indicates that there is a source from within the organism. I have quoted Blondel in Chapter Three (page seven) where he says that there is a source of action within the organism that unifies disparate events and factors.

The question then is. "Where do we locate this source of action?" And is the answer "In the brain"?, and then we go further and ask, "But where in the brain?" Neuroscientists now all say that actions cannot be located in any single factor in the brain but arise from a unified co-operation, yet where does this come from. Do we go back and say that its source is in the struggle for survival?

What is "value" though? When someone tells me that there is a value in doing something, I am being told that something is worth doing. The difference between Freud's "avoidance" and Macmurray's "value" is that the natural instinct is to avoid pain and enjoy pleasure. This is not something that someone decides to do. It is something that someone is driven to do. He or she is a passive slave of an impulse. Macmurray recommends the opposite of this when he says: "Freedom has a higher value than happiness; and this is what we recognize when we honour those who have been ready to sacrifice happiness, and even life itself, for freedom's sake."

There is the implication here of a higher purpose but what is it? And there is contained in this statement the view that the ego is able to transcend the instinctual impulse. How is this possible? It means that what differentiates living things from lifeless objects is that in the former there is a principle of action entirely from within whereas in the latter the source of action is entirely from the outside of the object. The billiard ball will only move when struck by the cue or another ball; the amoeba, however, will move towards a juicy morsel; there is a source of action from within itself. One can slowly travel up the genealogical tree of life from the simplest organism to the most complex, arriving in the end at *homo sapiens sapiens*. When we reach human beings there is something else present: awareness. Normally we are not aware of the activities governed by the autonomic nervous system, like breathing or our pulse, but we can become aware of them. Buddhism has cultivated this awareness, through meditation, of these basic life processes. Awareness registers the fact that there is a something in the organism that is separate from the life processes themselves.

Pain and pleasure are sensual occurrences striking the organism, to which it reacts. When Freud introduces the ego centre stage he does indicate that it is, as it were, the manager of both the outer and inner stimuli, so he introduces another source of action within the personality, within the planet.

But what do we mean when we say that something has a value? Someone might say of an experience that it was painful but then add that, however, there was a value in it. The person might say that it enlarged understanding or was helpful for a friend. Value always points to something which is beyond the sensual, beyond the material, beyond the immediate. It implies that there is a mental world whose governing principles are different from that of Freud's seeking of pleasure and avoidance of pain. But what is this "beyond"? It has to be something that is totally *in* what happens and yet is not it. Volume is totally in the bag of feathers or the bar of gold and yet is distinguishable from it. There is a principle that is totally *in* the human event and yet is separate from it. It is painful to have one's tooth drilled by the dentist and yet it has a value. We are bringing in another reality by which we make this judgment. In the case of the pain of the tooth being drilled we say that it is worth suffering because the tooth will therefore not decay. We speak of an act of generosity that has a value "in itself". What is implied here that it is not in terms of a reward. An act of generosity has a value even if it is not reciprocated. What is this "in itself"? There has to be a something in terms of which an action is recommended. Freud says, do the action if it leads to pleasure or avoids pain, but the act of generosity which may bring pain is then being praised for it goes counter to the hedonistic principle. There is thus the inference here that there are two principles governing human behaviour: one is informed by what is satisfying to the organism; the other is satisfying to some principle that is outside it.

There are two facts which are certain. One is that there is a universe which just is; the other is that I, the individual, did not exist at one time and came into existence at a definite historical point of time. That universe, that fact of existence, is something that has no cause. It just *is*. When we speak of a value that is in terms of something beyond the life preservative instincts of the organism, we are talking of the existence which *is* which requires no thrust to survive. Its existence just is and it is this that is immanent in the organism and makes sense of the word "value".

CHAPTER ELEVEN

When all-inclusive principles are diffuse

In Chapter Five I wrote of the way an all-inclusive principle permeates a range of elements in the personality. The problem is how to locate this principle when it is very diffuse. Grief is easy to detect when it is hitched to a particular event. At a funeral a wife is weeping as her husband's coffin is lowered into the grave, its final resting place. But say the grief is because Natalie's mother was depressed after giving birth to her. Depression means, in this case, that her mother was physically present but her spirit was absent after Natalie's birth. The loss of her mother's spirit caused grief, like the woman whose husband was being buried. Natalie's grief is intense but it cannot be linked to the event that has stimulated it, so it is diffused through the personality. I say that it *cannot* be linked but this is not quite right. It is with difficulty that it is linked. The two examples above illustrate the matter. In the case of the wife weeping as her husband's coffin is being lowered into the grave there is an inner connection between her and what is happening. It is possible for an inner connection to occur for Natalie also. It would be necessary for her to feel some feature in her personality and to see in a living way the connection to her absent mother. Let us say she has always had a longing to be loved by her brother but knowing always that this is not so. She has the sense of

131

her brother's absence and of seeing suddenly that this pre-dated her longing for her brother in a longing for her mother's love. A moment of illumination occurs that lights up several pathways in her life. I think it is something like this that Bion was trying to describe in his use of the term *the selected fact* where he says: "The selected fact is the name of an emotional experience, the emotional experience of a sense of discovery of coherence ..." (1984, p. 73). *Coherence* is the crucial word here. In Natalie's longing for her brother, in a moment a pathway of similar longing is lit up, leading to her mother. It is the longing as a principle which receives its essential colouring from her relation to her mother. At that moment the knowledge that her mother was depressed after her birth ceases to be a practical fact like there is a Statue of Liberty at the entrance to New York harbour or the Battle of Waterloo was fought in the year 1815. Instead this disposition known as "longing" becomes shot through with personal significance.

In fact grief as an emotion receives its character as grief through its relation to the stimulating event. This phrase "grief as an emotion" means an object communicating itself and being registered as a state which is called "grief". The Russian philosopher, Vladimir Solovyov, taught that the ethical character of an action is shaped by the object towards which the action tends: "... the quality of being virtuous or vicious depends upon a certain relation to the object and not on the psychological nature of the emotional and volitional states" (1918, p. 96). What he says ethically is also so emotionally. The crucial words here are "a certain relation to ...". This "relation to" is what is known as an emotion. There is a "relating to" which is an action but not a motor action. It is not a visible, material, measurable activity. It is the invisible activity that passes between one human being and another. This activity receives its colouring from the mode in which the action occurs. "Longing" is one colouring; "remembering" is another, and so on. Is grief good or bad? This, as has been observed in the previous chapter, depends upon what is assumed. On Freud's hedonistic principle it is bad but on Macmurray's principle it is good, but why? It is painful but achieving a good end. The good is the making of the external event into an inner possession. This is done through the work of an inner creative principle.

Until an event is "located" it cannot be named; it might be grief or disappointment. It depends for its particular colouring on the object and the relation to the object. It is the quality of this inner relation which alters the object and is altered by the object. There is an interrelation between the two which is never the same for two different people. An example is the way two different artists depict the same scene. A painting of Venice by Canaletto is very different from one painted by an impressionist. Something cannot be named until it has become differentiated. Grief has not become grief until it has separated and become differentiated from disappointment and humiliation. These three are an aggregate mass until they become differentiated. Water is not ice; it becomes ice when a certain temperature has been reached. The diffuse disposition might be one that could be described as melancholic but the particular principle may be disappointment, humiliation, despair, or frustration. What is met in the consulting room is an emotional state that is not easily defined but which permeates the individual's whole behaviour. It is a disposition.

Whenever I met Antoinette she complained about the way people treated her. Her friend, Agatha, had arranged to have lunch with her on Tuesday but rang and cancelled, saying that she was not well, but later Antoinette heard that Agatha had been quite well and had gone to see a film that day; Stanley told Antoinette of a cruise he had been on in the Caribbean and that it had cost $15,000 and asked why did she not also take such a cruise—it would cheer her up, but Stanley knew that she did not have available such a sum to spend; she arrived at the doctor's surgery at the appointed time but he had forgotten the appointment and was away. She told me these incidents one after another and every time I saw her she relayed to me more such events. What was the underlying disposition here? I would call it the *hard-done-by* disposition. A psychiatrist might call it depression. This *hard-done-by* disposition permeates all her activities. The *hard-done-by* state was an aggregate and its component parts—grief, disappointment, despair— had not yet become such. Differentiation and being the source of action are complementary to each other. Victimhood and aggregation of parts are also partners of one another. An institution is always a victim, never the source of action. A person is the source of action, never a victim.

It is not only emotional states which are congealed into one solid lump but also differences of time and place. So, for instance, the analyst's consulting room and her own home were amalgamated in her mind, as also were different times of day. It seems that emotional states, places, and times become aggregated. The primal forces here are the emotional states which, as a substrate, also govern times and places. They also become amalgamated and this is because emotion lies at the source of the personality. Emotion is the connecting link between one person and another and this is the foundation stone; it is what makes human community. Different classes of people also become congealed into one solid body when the emotional substrate remains undifferentiated. What we have to ask now is, "What is it that enables the differentiation?"

A relation which is entirely personal, that characterises these two people and their relation to each other, and being different to that of any other, is the catalyst which introduces differentiation of emotions within the personality. The outer mode of relating of one person to the other is a reflection of the mode of interrelation between parts within. Yet this expression is not right. There is no outer mode of relating. There is attachment of one to the other through the senses yet this is not relating but a fastening of one to the other like the gluing together of one piece of wood to another. Attachment through the senses is glue-like. Touch is the fundamental linking mode of the senses which governs seeing and hearing. Sensual seeing and hearing are an extended way of touching. One person *relating* to another is an entirely different process. One has first to posit that there is a reality in which both participate. There are certain core happenings which are common to all mankind. Every human has been born, every human has been entirely dependent upon another for a period of his or her life, every individual has needed another to bring his own potentials into actuality, every individual will die and has knowledge of this event, every individual has experienced loss, every individual has known humiliation. These life events exist in one of two forms: either they exist but remain uncreated or they undergo a creative process. This creative process occurs through a relation with the other. The two are one activity. It is not that the relation between two people causes creativity or that creativity causes the relationship to happen. They are one thing viewed from two different angles. We divide them into the categories "interpersonal" and "intrapsychic" but they are two different angles on one reality. This is why I wrote that the "outer mode" of relating is not correct. The interpersonal and intrapsychic are both inner. The core inner experiences are not confined within the circumference of what is named "the individual". They are universal and therefore exist in every human being in any part of the world and in any historical epoch. They are also the "relating elements" within the individual. Just as one individual can be attached to another or in relation to another so also one part can be either attached to another within the personality or in relation. It is a question of whether the relating mode is stronger than the attachment mode.

Through a relation which is personal between the analyst and patient, the diffuse emotional state becomes more and more focused. As the focus becomes more and more centred upon its target so the emotion becomes less diffuse and more defined. A generalised state known as depression clarifies as being grief. It might have clarified as being disappointment or as humiliation. It may have been a combination of all three which have now separated out. It is the originating stimulus that gives the emotion its specific definition.

So a loss of a significant figure generates the feeling of grief; loss of a wished-for aspiration generates disappointment, loss of hope generates despair. There are other specifics which, until located, beget melancholy. The essence of melancholia is that it is a mood whose stimulus is unknown. Freud described this clearly in *Mourning and Melancholia* (1917e).

The big unknowns are undeveloped functions. Consider the following:

Capacity to feel
Imagination
Memory
Sexuality
Ability to abstract
Knowledge of existence
Ability to relate (communication cord)
Ability to converse
Ability to think
Ability to unify.

We often think that these are so elemental to the make-up of a human being that we do not consider that they can be absent or to exist in a very undeveloped state. The capacity to feel for another is such a function. Yet we are quite aware that someone may be physically blind, but not so conscious that someone may be blind to the presence of other people in the world, may be blind to his or her own existence.

There is a kind of double consciousness which makes it particularly difficult for us to realise blindness of this kind. There is knowledge which comes through the senses. I know I have an appointment with

Dr Camillo on Thursday at three in the afternoon at 99 Resistance Road, Sydney in the borough of Breakdown, but emotionally he does not exist. I posit here two sources of information: one is through the senses and the other is through intuition. The words "Dr Camillo, Thursday 3.00 pm" are both received through the senses and transcribed through the senses. The diary in which these words are written is also an object taken in through the senses. His existence as a person separate from me is taken in through intuition. Intuition is a creative act. I create the other. This needs further elaboration.

The reality of being is known through a personal act, through a creative act. I cannot teach it to someone. In the same way that gravity existed before Newton so also being exists but is not known by a human mind until it is grasped. I think this is what Wilfred Bion is referring to when he says:

> If there is a thing-in-itself, a thing which Kant would call the nou-menon, all that we can know is about phenomena. When the nou-mena, the things themselves, push forward so far that they meet an object which we can call a human mind there comes into being the domain of phenomena. (1974, p. 41)

He expresses this passively: "… the noumena … push forward so far that they meet an object which we can call a human mind." But the human mind is not a passive receptacle.

Yes, the noumena may push forward towards a mind but the mind also pushes forward. But we have to take in the idea that the world, including the self, is a congealed mass. Paradoxically it is the creative act which separates. I say "paradoxically" because the creative act grasps the whole of being but, and this is mysterious, the creative act catches the principle and only from that act does individual variety flow. The One and the Many has always been, and always will be, a philosophical conundrum. Spinoza, whose philosophy was founded upon Substance or God, as he called it, could not explain variety. He introduced the idea of "modes" of this substance but how, out of this oneness, are these differences possible? Yet it is so. Variety we know through the senses; oneness we know through an act of intellect. But the point I am wanting to stress is that this latter is an entirely personal act. Someone can teach his pupil about this tree, that porcupine, this house, that stretch of water but he cannot teach the oneness, he cannot teach Substance. This has to be grasped through an act of understanding. The source of this act is entirely in the person. This is because the person is the Substance. Substance knows itself. Substance is intellect. The intellect is Substance knowing itself. Bion stressed the need to suppress memory and desire but it is more than that. It is the suppression of sense experience of which memory and desire are particular expressions. When I have an act of understanding it is a case of substance knowing itself. Memory and desire get in the way of this but also self-assertion. This is an assertion of oneself against Substance. It is a blinding of Substance. It takes the focus away from the oneness of things. The religious idea of dying to self is a precondition for an act of understanding. But this is because Substance can only come to be if the focus of attention is upon it. And it is in this *it* that the self and the other have their true being. But in this personal grasping is contained the "otherness" of the other. Through this lens we are able to see the other as he or she is and not as he or she "ought" to be. This "oughtness" comes from a failure of the personal act.

I want to elaborate this a little more: there are two truths of which I am completely certain. The first is that there is a universe—so vast that it is beyond the capacity of our imagination to visualise it. To cross our own galaxy, just one of millions, yes, just to cross from one end to the other of our own galaxy takes 60,000 light years. Something so vast that it is incomprehensible and yet this is just one of hundreds of billions of galaxies swirling around in the vastness of space. I remember a philosopher friend saying that sometimes he woke at night and imagined going in a spacecraft to the very end of the universe and there meeting a high wall and he would climb up it and look over but there on the other side was nothing: no thing but he would keep seeing a shadowy something. Imagination is of something so it is a useless instrument when it comes to an absence. A favourite author in my youth was G. K. Chesterton and he understood this well:

> The imagination is supposed to work towards the infinite; though in that sense the infinite is the opposite of imagination. For the imagination deals with an image. And an image is in its nature a thing that has an outline and therefore a limit. (1938, p. 107)

The mind cannot represent an absence—there is, as my philosopher friend said, always "a shadowy something". Representation is of a thing and therefore is stumped when it comes to a "no thing". So how does the mind get around this difficulty? It fashions a monster. The savage superego is such a monster. The monster then tells me: "See, you're useless, you're hopeless, you don't deserve to exist." This is because it is a crude instrument with no capacity to differentiate.

And it is very unpopular if someone comes up to me and says: "You know Neville, you haven't got the capacity to think," or "You haven't got the capacity to imagine," or "You haven't got the capacity to feel for somebody." I do not like that. I am sort of ashamed of that yet it is necessary to try to isolate the function that is undeveloped and speak about it. This requires tact and care due to the shame there is. My experience is that if that can happen and that function begins to develop, the monster begins to decrease and the personality begins to feel more okay about itself. It is only then I think too, when the basic functions are operating reasonably well, that it is possible in a creative act to bring them into a unity. They cannot be brought into a unity when there is one function that is undeveloped. And consciousness, there is such a rash of literature at the moment from physicists, other scientists, neuroscientists, psychologists, sociologists—everyone is into consciousness. It may be over-simple but I think that consciousness is that unity. Consciousness is when that unity is present.

Accidental happenings, chance encounters—these are a big actor on the human stage but we humans do not like to think that we, this important species, can be the casualties of pure chance. We read intentionality into events that do not merit it. Henri Bergson, whom I mentioned as an influence in Chapter One, makes this interesting statement:

> The extremely varied examples of "primitive mentality" which M. Lévy-Bruhl has accumulated in his works can be grouped under a certain number of headings. The most numerous are those which show, according to the author, that primitive man obstinately refuses to admit the existence of chance. If a stone falls and crushes a passer-by, it was an evil spirit that dislodged it: there is no chance about it. If a man is dragged out of his canoe by an alligator, it is because he was bewitched: there is no chance about it. If a warrior is killed or wounded by lance-thrust, it is because he was not in a state to parry the blow, a spell had been cast upon him: there was

no chance about it … when you reproach primitive man with not believing in chance … are you quite sure that you are not relapsing into that primitive mentality which you criticize … A huge tile, wrenched off by the wind, falls and kills a passer-by. We say it was chance. Should we say the same if the tile had merely crashed onto the ground? (1935, p. 123).

Wilfred Bion, in his characteristic way, said on one occasion that we had not yet recovered from the Battle of Marathon. The Battle of Marathon occurred 2,500 years ago. What I am wanting to emphasise here is that even when there is an accidental event it gets endowed, as Bergson notes, with human intentionality, but it happens all the more so when the event is being relayed through the agency of human beings.

It is only my own personal emotional thinking that gets through the tyrannical barrier and reaches the personhood buried within the steel corset of a superego tyranny. I had the good fortune early in my psycho-analytic career to meet up with a patient who taught me this. Once or twice she said to me, "Is that what you think or what you have learned to think?" I will quote to you an intriguing example which Marion Milner gives us:

> … after many years of writing, I had finally found people to teach me who did see that the essence of painting is that every mark on the paper should be one's own, growing out of the uniqueness of one's own psycho-physical structure and experience, not a mechanical copy of the model, however skilful. Incidentally I showed this book to a painter, who, while turning over the pages to look at the drawings said, "That one is not you, nor that, nor that, they are unconscious copies of some picture you have seen." I had myself recognized the obvious derivation of Mrs Punch from the Duchess in *Alice's Adventures in Wonderland*, just as the chair in *Nursery* derived from van Gogh; and also that the design in the *Blasting Witch* was a close unconscious copy of the design of a picture I had often seen in a friend's room. But the painter had never seen this friend's picture and it was a surprise to me that anyone could know, without having seen the "copy", that the line of the drawing was not my own, not growing out of my own psycho-physical rhythms. Of the wavy line at the top left side of *The Eagle and the Cave-man* he said,

"That is good, that is from you; though the shading is not, that is mannered, banal." The point of view prompting these criticisms confirmed my growing conviction that a work of art, whatever its content, or subject, whether a recognizable scene or object or abstract pattern, must be an externalization, through its shapes and lines and colours, of the unique psycho-physical rhythm of the person making it. Otherwise it will have no life in it whatever, for there is no other source of life. (1987, p. 230)

I think that these functions come to life through recognition of them and love of them by the mother. The mother who is differentiated in her own functions is able to recognise the particular gifts of each of her children.

What does the analyst need to do to bring about this transformation? What is it about his mode of being towards the patient that enables it? There is a sense here that the individual needs to find the originating stimulus. So this means that it is there but needs to be discovered. But we have already observed that it is not truly there until it has come into contact with the stimulating object. But how is this possible? Natalie's emotion is in this diffuse state and the stimulating object is not present. But she is now in relation to someone. He refers to himself as a psychoanalyst. He is involved in a three stage process: participation, observation, and creation. These three are interconnected.

The core of life is transformative. This is how evolution has happened. It is why in the seventh chapter I emphasised the need to incorporate Lamarck into our thinking about evolution. So, for instance, at the heart of Darwin's conception is the mating of a random mutation within the organism with the thrust for survival. Random mutation mates with a factor favoured by the environment. So it is two blind factors mating to the organism's benefit. There is no instrument of transformation in this model. However, Lamarck believed that life in its essence was transformative and this is how new species have arisen; that there is an intelligent learning going on in an individual organism and that this can be passed from the *soma* to the gene pool.

The answer, we realise, lies partly in our definition of the person: that the person, as opposed to the individual, is an organisation with a centering principle that holds the whole together in a unity. The unity in one invites it in the other. It is as Bonhoeffer says: "… the call of human existence to unity with itself" (1970, p. 242).

The personhood in the one invites the other to personhood. This unity in the one stimulates desire in the other.

Participation

There is a reality in which the analyst and the patient participate. This is the reality which Bion referred to as "O". Otherwise they could not be in relation to one another. Bion defines O thus: "I shall use the sign *O* to denote that which is the ultimate reality represented by terms such as ultimate reality, absolute truth, the godhead, the infinite, the thing-in-itself" (1970, p. 26). Because patient and analyst participate in this reality they are in relation to one another. This reality in which they both participate is not grasped through the senses. As Tolstoy says: "The most fundamental consciousness of being is not received through the senses, for there is no special organ to convey that consciousness" (1986, p. 37).

It is grasped through what Aquinas called an act of intellect and what Bion called intuition. It is also what Picasso referred to as the "inner eye" (Penrose, 1971, pp. 91–92). This has already been referred to in Chapter One and again in Chapter Four. Picasso locates this unity at the point of junction between sensual perception and the deeper regions of the mind. Whereas Plato located the human being's essence in the soul, Aquinas located it in the junction between mind and body which Picasso does also. Aquinas arrives at it through his Christian belief linked to the philosophy of Aristotle but Picasso arrives at it through his own personal experience of artistic observation.

It is the reality of O that enables a relationship. Klauber emphasised that the relationship is neglected in psychoanalytic discourse: "The most neglected feature of the psychoanalytic relationship still seems to me to be that it is a relationship …" (1981, p. 46).

So the patient is in relation to the analyst. A relationship is a connection existing between two people. The analyst as stimulating object localises what is diffuse in such a way that depression can become grief (or disappointment or despair). It can be named when it assumes a shape.

The implication here is that the relationship is capable of transforming diffuseness into a defined shape. When it has a shape it can be named. A premature naming can crush the emerging shape. For there to be a relationship the analyst's first task is to define himself. For the diffuseness in the patient to assume a form the analyst has himself to have a shape, around which or in relation to which a form can begin to evolve in the patient. It evolves also in the analyst.

The relationship is something that happens when two people inhabit the same localised space: the human correlate of gravitational attraction that exists between any two physical objects.

Observation

The analyst's task then is to observe "instances of similarity" arising in the communication. Now, an important principle needs to be invoked here: it is that what is there needs to be created. It is that although something is there yet it needs to be created to become found. When Isaac Newton discovered gravity it was a creative act. He created it, yet it was already there. In a similar way a grief which is in the personality has to be created. This creation can only occur through a relation to another which is personal. Something can be created in me through the creative agency of another. How is this to occur?

EPILOGUE

The residence of the "it", the uncreated, the non-person, is the institution. Institutions are made up of "its"—uncreated elements. Institutions embody rules and regulations, formulated by committees in the hope that the spirit which initiated a movement of thought will be maintained by succeeding generations, yet frequently the maintainers of institutions do not have the spirit of the founder but rather an ingestion of a series of non-personal regulations. That profound Russian thinker Vladimir Solovyov, who was in no way a cynic said: "Institutions which ought to serve the good in humanity may more or less deviate from their purpose or even be wholly false to it" (1918, p. 177). This is why people with an obsessional neurotic character structure find a familiar home in the institution. Obsessional neurosis is the spiritless institution within the character of the individual. So this embodiment exists both outside the individual and also within and it crushes the creative principle at the heart of the personality. The individual may be efficient, and loyal to the institution, but that which it was supposed to serve instead strangles the life in the person. Using an analogy from the central nervous system we might say that the personal, the creative principle is situated in the *old brain* and the institutional group in the *new brain*.

143

The institution comprises all in our world that precedes the birth of this individual, and thus language, cities, banks, museums, transport facilities, scientific knowledge are all components of the organisational enterprise. The latter embraces all the discoveries in astronomy, evolution, and medicine, and the principles governing the movement of bodies such as gravity, genetics, and so on. We are all creatures of a world where this accumulated knowledge exists as a fact. This is the institutional world into which we are born and which finds through learning a residence in the outer layers of our minds. These facts are, however, never correct. As the history of scientific discovery teaches us, something that was taught as a definite fact becomes disproved through the creative insight of future scientists. So, for instance, Copernicus displaced the Ptolemaic system with his own personal insight. So also Lavoisier displaced the phlogiston theory, and so on.

These established institutional facts are inwardly clung to with intensity. It is such intense clinging which fashions this reality into what analytical discourse has named the superego. This was first outlined by Freud, further elaborated by Melanie Klein, and given the institutional breadth by Talcott Parsons.

Violet Bonham Carter, writing of Churchill, whom she believed was a genius, said:

> I felt also that the impact of life, ideas and even words upon his mind was not only vivid and immediate, but *direct*. Between him and them there was no shock-absorber of vicarious thought or precedent gleaned either from books or other minds. His relationship with all experience was first-hand. (1966, pp. 16–17)

The same thing has been said of other geniuses. A. N. Wilson in his 1988 biography of Tolstoy wrote that he had a hypersensitivity to his surroundings, which is another way of saying the same thing. The genius will often also recommend to others that they enter into direct contact with their own experience. Kant used to encourage his students to think for themselves. Before the Buddha was dying he told his disciples not to rely on what he had said but to test things for themselves. Bion (1961) also emphasised the primacy of one's own experience and further he believed that there is in us a hatred of it. Freud (1912e) also makes the same point. There is a violent reluctance to enter into a first-hand relation with one's own experience. So a differentiation is being made here between direct experience as opposed to illusion which is indirect.

So what do we mean by illusion which is indirect? Violet Bonham Carter (1966) gives the clue when she refers to "vicarious thought". She also infers that this gives the individual a protective barrier—"there was no shock-absorber" in her chosen genius.

So how do I envelop myself with this protective shield? I can either take the thinking of another and cloak myself within it or propel myself into it. There are two questions here: why? and how?

To be in direct contact with experience condemns someone to a life of both inner agony and sublime joy, but this is a sore trial for any individual. It also puts pressure on the person to be constantly rearranging the inner template of his existence. There is a current of thinking in some psychoanalytic literature that puts forward the notion that *equilibrium* is what is wanted. This is endorsed by what Freud, following Fechner (see Ellenberger, 1970), referred to as the *principle of constancy*, and then known as the *homeostatic principle* as formulated by W. B. Cannon (see Hilgard & Atkinson, 1967). This is a recommendation to eschew genius. The geniuses like Shakespeare, Raphael, Copernicus, Isaac Newton, Pasteur, Tolstoy, Gandhi, Churchill, Darwin, Marx, Freud, or Bion have allowed the genius to come to full flower within them. We lesser mortals cannot manage this degree of intensity in our feeble frames but we can tend the gentle plant within us. This is what Kant is recommending to his students. He did not prescribe *balance or equilibrium*. The genius has been dedicated to the truth which is ever a bearer of *discomfort, disequilibrium*, or *imbalance*. We avoid the genius within us because it presages *discomfort*. I think this is why we propel ourselves into the thinking of another and embrace discipleship. It is like a cloak which we wrap around ourselves giving us *comfort* and *equilibrium*, but quite why does it do so? It is because the genius has confronted life *directly* but we, his disciples, follow him. Tolstoy once said of someone who had come to visit him: "He is a Tolstoyan, that is a man with convictions utterly opposed to mine" (Wilson, 1988, p. 452). He would have meant, I believe, that whereas Tolstoy himself believed in connecting directly with life itself his visitor followed what Tolstoy said and did.

So this, I believe, is *why* we do it but then the question is how. There are two forms of projection. First the kind where I project a part of myself into a suitable receptacle and second where I project my whole self or my central self, to use Fairbairn's term, into a fitting repository. This is well expressed through Vernon, a character in George Meredith's *The Egoist*: "Vernon turned from the portraits to a stuffed pike in a glass-case, and plunged into sympathy with the fish for a refuge" (1919, p. 270).

George Meredith here clearly knows the way in which someone can find refuge by "plunging into sympathy with". In this case it was with a stuffed pike. I think George Meredith knew intuitively that Vernon could "plunge into sympathy with" a stuffed pike which would not have been possible with a portrait. A fish, a three dimensional fish although a stuffed one, can be "plunged into" because the man and the fish share the three dimensional quality. I think this notion of "plunging into sympathy with" gets us closer to the *how*. It is impossible to think of projecting oneself into something which has no equivalent substance to oneself. Henri Bergson has described the way in which there is a sympathy between living substances. However, to subscribe to such a view requires one to think of the self as a fluid entity. We tend to think of ourselves as a solid something but this idea of sympathy suggests that this other object and myself share a substance. Once there is a shared substance there can be an exchange.

But what is the situation when I have not projected myself into something which acts as a protective cloak? When there is no shock-absorber between me and the reality itself? I think here one has to posit that there are two modes of action—discharge and acceptance. Discharge leads to an impoverishment of the mind whereas acceptance—and this means acceptance of the changing movements of the tectonic plates within—enriches the capacity to see directly into the surrounding world.

In Chapter Eight I said I would return to the question of the brain's evolution to the point at which it could enable the mind to have reverie or to represent. Freud had the idea of free floating attention and Bion had the idea of reverie, which are similar, and the idea that the mother processes the anxiety coming from the baby and transforms it and gives it back in an acceptable form. I have no complaint with that but I think contemplation is something a bit deeper than that. If you think of the mother with the infant, she is contemplating her baby and this contemplative act embraces the whole world, of which this baby is a living part. So contemplation is more active than free floating attention or reverie. Contemplation is the goal of which meditation is the preparation; like sexual intercourse is the goal for which foreplay is the preparation. The contemplative act reaches through from one person to the other. It goes from centre to centre, penetrating right through the outer. This is why sexual intercourse is a fitting analogy for the way in which one person interpenetrates with another. This analogy to sexual intercourse would be pleasing to Freud. And here we finish.

REFERENCES

Aries, P. (1960). *Centuries of Childhood*. London: Penguin, 1962.

Aristotle. *Ethics*. Book 8 Ch. 5. London: Penguin, 1955.

Balkanyi, C. (1964). On verbalization. *International Journal of Psychoanalysis*, 45: 64–74.

Bergson, H. (1911). *Creative Evolution*. London: Macmillan, 1919.

Bergson, H. (1935). *The Two Sources of Morality and Religion*. London: Macmillan.

Berlin, I. (1979). Against the current. In: *Vico's Concept of Knowledge*. London: Hogarth.

Bick, E. (1986). Further considerations on the function of the skin in early object relations. In: A. Briggs (Ed.), *Surviving Space—Papers on Infant Observation*. London: Karnac, 2002.

Bion, W. R. (1961). *Experiences in Groups*. London: Tavistock.

Bion, W. R. (1962). *Learning from Experience*. London: Karnac, 1984.

Bion, W. R. (1963). *Elements of Psychoanalysis*. London: Karnac, 1989.

Bion, W. R. (1970). *Attention and Interpretation*. London: Tavistock.

Bion, W. R. (1974). *Bion's Brazilian Lectures, vol. 1*. Rio de Janeiro: Imago Editora.

Birch, C. (1995). *Feelings*. Sydney: University of New South Wales Press.

Bléandonu, G. (1994). *Wilfred Bion*. London: Free Association.

Blondel, M. (1893). *Action*. Notre Dame, IN: University of Notre Dame Press, 1984.

Bonham Carter, V. (1966). *Winston Churchill as I Knew Him*. London: The Reprint Society.

Bonhoeffer, D. (1970). *Ethics*. London: Collins, Fontana Library.

Bryant, A. (1969). *The Lion and the Unicorn*. London: Collins.

Buber, M. (1937). *I and Thou*. 2nd edition. R. G. Smith (Trans.). Edinburgh: T. & T. Clark, 1987.

Chesterton, G. K. (1905). *Heretics*. London: Bodley Head.

Chesterton, G. K. (1910). *What's Wrong with the World*. London: Cassell.

Chesterton, G. K. (1938). *Autobiography*. London: Hutchinson.

Cicero. Laelius: On Friendship. In: *Cicero on the Good Life* (pp. 204–205). London: Penguin, 1984.

Damasio, A. (2003). *Looking for Spinoza*. London: William Heinemann.

Dennett, D. C. (1993). *Consciousness Explained*. London: Penguin.

Dilthey, W. (1989). The Facts of Consciousness ("Brelau Draft"). In: *Selected Works—Introduction to the Human Sciences* (pp. 287–288). Princeton, NJ: Princeton University Press.

Eckhart, Meister. *Selected Treatises and Sermons*. Collins, Fontana Library, 1963.

Eckhart, Meister. *The Essential Sermons, Commentaries, Treatises and Defense*. E. Colledge & B. McGinn (Trans.). Mahwah, NJ: Paulist, 1981.

Eliot, G. (1874). *Middlemarch*. London: Penguin, 1973.

Ellenberger, H. F. (1970). *The Discovery of the Unconscious*. London: Allen Lane/Penguin.

Ferro, A. (2005). *Seeds of Illness, Seeds of Recovery*. P. Slotkin (Trans.). Hove, UK: Brunner-Routledge.

Freud, S. (1912e). Recommendations to physicians practising psycho-analysis. *S. E., 12*. London: Hogarth.

Freud, S. (1913i). The disposition to obsessional neurosis. *S. E., 12*. London: Hogarth.

Freud, S. (1914d). On the history of the psycho-analytic movement. *S. E., 14*. London: Hogarth.

Freud, S. (1915d). Repression. *S. E., 14*. London: Hogarth.

Freud, S. (1915e). The unconscious. *S. E., 14*. London: Hogarth.

Freud, S. (1917e). Mourning and melancholia. *S. E., 14*. London: Hogarth.

Freud, S. (1919a). Lines of advance in psycho-analytic therapy. *S. E., 17*. London: Hogarth.

Freud, S. (1923b). *The Ego and the Id. S. E., 19*. London: Hogarth.

Freud, S. (1930a). *Civilization and its Discontents. S. E., 21*. London: Hogarth.

Freud, S. (1940b). Some elementary lessons in psycho-analysis. *S. E.*, *23*. London: Hogarth.

Grossman, V. (1995). *Life and Fate*. London: Harvill Press.

Harré, H. R. (1983). *Personal Being*. Oxford: Blackwell.

Hilgard, E. R. & Atkinson, R. C. (1967). *Introduction to Psychology*. 4th edition. New York: Harcourt, Brace & World.

Hobson, P. (2002). *The Cradle of Thought*. London: Macmillan.

Honeywill, R. (2008). *Lamarck's Evolution*. Sydney, Australia: Murdoch/ Pier 9.

Jones, E. (1972). *Sigmund Freud—Life and Work, vol*. 1. London: Hogarth.

Jung, C. G. (1963). *Memories, Dreams, Reflections*. London: Flamingo, Fontana Paperbacks, 1977.

Kelley, C. F. (1977). *Meister Eckhart on Divine Knowledge*. New Haven, CT: Yale University Press.

Klauber, J. (1981). *Difficulties in the Analytic Encounter*. New York: Jason Aronson.

Laplanche, J. & Pontalis, J.-B. (1973). *The Language of Psycho-analysis*. London: Hogarth and Institute of Psycho-Analysis.

Lhote, A. (1998). *Classic Cézanne*. Art Gallery of New South Wales: Thames and Hudson.

Macmurray, J. (1949). *Conditions of Freedom*. Toronto, Canada: Ryerson.

Macneile Dixon, W. (1958). *The Human Situation*. London: Penguin.

Mann, P. & Mann, S. (2008). *Sargy Mann. Probably the Best Blind Painter in Peckham*. London: SP Books.

March, P. (2004). *The Mind as Relation.* (Privately circulated.)

McCann, Abbot J. (Ed.) (1952). *The Cloud of Unknowing and Other Treatises by an English Mystic of the Fourteenth Century*. London: Burns Oates.

Meredith, G. (1919). *The Egoist*. London: Constable.

Milner, M. (1934). *A Life of One's Own*. London: Virago, 1986.

Milner, M. (1937). *An Experiment in Leisure*. Los Angeles, CA: J. P. Tarcher, 1987.

Milner, M. (1987). *The Suppressed Madness of Sane Men*. London: Tavistock.

Mithen, S. (1996). *The Prehistory of the Mind*. London: Thames & Hudson.

Montaigne, M. de (1991). *On the Power of the Imagination*. In: M. A. Screech (Trans.), *The Complete Essays* (pp. 109–120). London: Penguin.

Newman, J. H. (1875). *Parochial and Plain Sermons, vol. III*. London: Rivingtons.

Newman, J. H. (1927). *The Idea of a University*. New York: Longmans, Green.

Off, C. (2008). *Bitter Chocolate*. St Lucia, Australia: University of Queensland Press.

Ogden, T. H. (2009). *Rediscovering Psychoanalysis*. London: Routledge, New Library of Psychoanalysis.

Orwell, G. (1957). *Shooting an Elephant*. In: Inside the Whale and Other *Essays*. London: Penguin.

Parsons, T. (1964). *Social Structure and Personality*. London: Free Press, 1970.

Penrose, R. (1971). *Picasso*. London: Penguin.

Polanyi, M. (1959). *The Study of Man*. Chicago, IL: University of Chicago Press.

Shirley-Price, L. (Trans.) (1959). *The Little Flowers of St. Francis*. London: Penguin.

Shulman, D. (2005). *Is the Artist's Imagination Free? A View from Mediaeval India*. (Privately circulated.)

Soames, M. (Ed.) (1999). *Speaking for Themselves. The Personal Letters of Winston and Clementine Churchill*. (Letter of 20 December 1915.) London: Black Swan.

Sobel, D. (1998). *Longitude*. London: Fourth Estate.

Solovyov, V. (1918). *The Justification of the Good*. London: Constable's Russian Library.

Streeter, B. H. (1935). *Reality*. London: Macmillan.

Suttie, I. D. (1939). *The Origins of Love and Hate*. London: Kegan Paul, Trench, Trübner.

Symington, N. (2002). *A Pattern of Madness*. London: Karnac.

Symington, N. (2004). *The Blind Man Sees*. London: Karnac.

Tillich, P. (1964a). *The Courage to Be*. London: Collins, Fontana Library.

Tillich, P. (1964b). *The Shaking of the Foundations*. London: Penguin.

Tillich, P. (1973). *Boundaries of Our Being*. Collins, Fontana Library.

Tolstoy, L. N. (1869). *War and Peace*. London: Penguin, 1986.

Tolstoy, L. N. (1877). *Anna Karenina*. R. Edmonds (Trans.). London: Penguin, 1986.

Tolstoy, L. N. (1899). What is art? In: *The Complete Works of Lyof N. Tolstoi* (pp. 1–203). New York: Thomas Y. Crowell.

Turnbull, C. (1961). *The Forest People*. London: Granada, Triad Paladin.

Vygotsky, L. S. (1962). *Thought and Language*. Cambridge, MA: MIT Press, 1975.

Warnock, M. (1979). *Existentialism*. Oxford: Oxford University Press.

Whitehead, A. F. (1958). *An Introduction to Mathematics*. Oxford: Oxford University Press.

Wilson, A. N. (1988). *Tolstoy*. London: Hamish Hamilton.

INDEX

Penrose, R. 12, 141
perception 83
periodic creationism 102
person
    analysis creating 1–13
    individual and 12
    organisations crushing the
        105–118
    resistance to becoming 91–103
personality, and love 94–103
Polanyi, Michael 9–10, 22, 31,
    74, 85
Pontalis, J.-B. 109
pragmatic knowledge 112–113
pratyabhijna 57–59
primary maternal preoccupation
    114
problems, historical determination
    of 77–90
puritanism 79

realisation, representation and
    27–28
relatedness 46
relating and clinging modes 45
representation and realisation
    27–28
repression 88–89, 109–110
    of sexuality 79–80, 87–88
reverie 110, 146
ritual burial 16

screen memories 32–33
seeing 108
    and hearing 134
selected fact, the 132
self-expression, Freudian conception
    of 43
sensations 42, 83
separation 21
sexual desires 77–78, 88–89, 109

sexuality, repression of 79–80, 82,
    87–88
shame 43–44, 46, 74
Shirley-Price, L. 117
Shulman, D. ix–x, 58
Siddhartha 112
Simantini story, précis of 56–61
slavophiles 44
Soames, M. 95
Sobel, D. 101
solidarity, principle of 45
Solovyov, Vladimir 30, 38, 43–45, 75,
    132, 143
speech and verbalization 19
Spinoza, B. 136
spiritual reality 46
stimulus-response theory of
    motivation 92
Streeter, B. H. 85–86
subjective function 40
sublimation 25
substance 137
superego, concept of 89
Suttie, I. D. 42–43
Symington, N. 7, 69
Synod of Paris 79

tabula rasa 117
The Egoist 47
The Epistle of Privy Counsel 125
The Interpretation of Dreams
    126
Tillich, P. 20, 73–74, 84, 98–99
Tolstoy, L. N. 8, 19, 25–26, 141,
    145
touch 134
tragedy, aspect of 99–102
transitive and formative power 58
Trinity 116
turbulence, pain and 91–94
Turnbull, C. 109